THE REAL ESTATE PROCESS

Pros Discuss
Buying & Selling Your Home

AUTHOR & EDITOR
Vi Brown, B.A.

CO-AUTHORS
Kelly Orr, LL.B.
Robert Hughes
Josée Lalonde

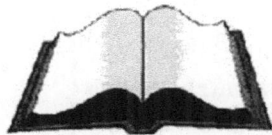

CCB Publishing
British Columbia, Canada

The Real Estate Process: Pros Discuss Buying & Selling Your Home

Copyright ©2010 by Vi Brown, B.A.
ISBN-13   978-1-926585-77-2
First Edition

Library and Archives Canada Cataloguing in Publication

Brown, Vi
The real estate process : pros discuss buying & selling your home /
author & editor, Vi Brown ; co-authors, Kelly Orr, Robert Hughes, Josée Lalonde.
-- 1st ed.
ISBN 978-1-926585-77-2
Also available in electronic format.
1. House buying. 2. House selling. 3. Real estate business. I. Title.
HD1379.B77 2010   643'.12   C2010-901591-6

Publisher: CCB Publishing
             British Columbia, Canada
             www.ccbpublishing.com

Dedication

This book is dedicated to all those

who are thinking of buying or selling a home

but don't know exactly where to begin!

Contents

Acknowledgments

When I finally decided to write about the real estate process, I felt that restricting it simply to my own input was not sufficient. The consumer deals with many professionals throughout the process and I wanted to incorporate their views and experience.

After much thought and planning, I made my first call to Kelly Orr at Browne Associates. I had met Kelly some years ago when I suggested to my client that we need to consult a lawyer regarding a very lengthy and complicated contract of purchase and sale. I was so highly impressed with the time and the manner with which she explained the legalities that her name immediately came to mind as a participant for this project. Kelly co-authored two chapters - the legal process involved in buying a home and also selling a home.

Next I contacted Robert Hughes, owner of Fleetwood Building Inspections, a man with an excellent reputation among my real estate colleagues. He has an easy manner about him and works well with his clients. He is organized, thorough and knows his stuff -- the right man for the job. Robert co-authored the home inspection chapter.

I wanted to incorporate a more recent discipline in real estate that is becoming increasingly more popular because of its effectiveness - home staging. Enter Josée Lalonde whose business is entitled Josée Lalonde Real Estate Staging. Without question she is creative and passionate about her work but she is also practical. She is the co-author of the home staging chapter.

It has been an absolute delight to work with all three of my co-authors. They are the consummate professionals. Their participation provides the consumer with added insight into the real estate process.

I would also like to extend my thanks to Alicia Fowler. At various times, she has worked as my assistant and has a general understanding of the real estate process but Alicia also has the 'ears' of a consumer.

I have asked her to read various segments of my manuscript - sometimes more than once or even more than twice! She has provided me with invaluable feedback. I am very grateful for her help.

Preface

Trademarks

Throughout this book, I use the terms REALTOR®, MLS® and Multiple Listing Service®. Every time these trademarks are used, they must be accompanied by the following statements.

"The trademarks REALTOR®, REALTORS®, and the REALTOR® logo are controlled by The Canadian Real Estate Association (CREA) and identify real estate professionals who are members of CREA. Used under license"

"The trademarks MLS®, Multiple Listing Service® and the associated logos are owned by The Canadian Real Estate Association (CREA) and identify the quality of services provided by real estate professionals who are members of CREA. Used under license"

Since it is not practical to insert these statements throughout the book because of their frequent usage, the above statements are implied.

Because REALTORS® are members of the Canadian Real Estate Association, this allows us to have access to the Multiple Listing Service®, or MLS®, the most complete and powerful listing service available. The MLS® Systems are financially supported by their memberships.

It does not follow that all real estate agents are REALTORS®. If they do not belong to a real estate board that is a member of CREA, they are simply real estate agents and not REALTORS®. As such, they do not have access to the MLS® Services.

REALTOR® - Definition

Throughout Canada, there are almost 100,000 REALTORS®/brokerages working within over 100 real estate boards and associations.

REALTORS® subscribe to CREA's Standards of Business Practice and The Code of Ethics. As such, you, the consumer, have the right to expect the highest professional standard of conduct and the best of service. It also requires that you are competently represented and that our dealings display the highest level of integrity and fairness.

This includes continued mandatory education to ensure competence and effectiveness.

The Code doesn't gather dust in some archive but is alive and well! Any complaints from the consumer are taken very seriously and are immediately addressed by the respective local real estate boards. Depending on the severity and complexity of the complaint, it may be elevated to a higher level of authority.

Guidelines to Consider

I and my co-authors are based in Victoria, British Columbia, Canada. As such, we are governed and must follow the specific guidelines of our respective provincial/federal associations.

Even though some of the contents of this book, such as terminology and forms used, are specific to a jurisdiction, there are ample general concepts discussed that can be most helpful across jurisdictions.

The intent of this book is not to provide you with all the answers with respect to buying and selling real estate. It is to provide you with an understanding of the general principles involved in the real estate process. In turn, this will enable you to proceed with greater confidence and empower you to ask the appropriate questions of professionals in your particular province or jurisdiction.

Introduction

Is This Real Estate Book Necessary?

That's a fair question. And the answer is a resounding –YES – !

As REALTORS®, we are always engaged in explaining some aspect of the real estate process to consumers who are thinking of buying or selling. This can take place in our office when they are ready to buy or sell or simply in a social setting because they know that's what we do.

There is nothing in the market place that addresses the real estate process itself. There are pieces of information everywhere. Almost every REALTOR® and financial institution can provide you with some information. There are even books addressing various elements of buying and selling homes but from the investment point of view and not the real estate process itself.

It is an overwhelming task for the consumer who wishes to buy or sell a home to collect this information and try to find some logical order that would actually provide some direction. If I'm a first time home buyer or if it has been years since I purchased, where do I begin. Do I go to my bank? Do I go to a REALTOR®? What do mortgage brokers do? How much can I afford? How will I know I have made a good buy?

If I want to sell my home, should I sell it myself? What is my home worth? Should I speak to a REALTOR®? Will I need a lawyer? How do I prepare my home for sale?

The purpose of this book is to connect the dots between all the elements of the real estate process and to have greater knowledge of each step. You will have the benefit of experienced professionals involved in the major steps of the process to provide you with their insights and how they can be of help along the way.

As you read through this book, you will find out more about each profession, the professionals and what they are actually doing to contribute to the process of your real estate purchase or sale. What should you be aware of and what questions should you be asking along the way. There are implications to each step of the process and many of these areas will be addressed.

Understanding all the elements of the real estate process and how they connect will empower you, the consumer, to make informed selections and decisions. This is critical because, whether you are buying or selling, you are making one of the largest financial decisions of your lifetime.

Required Documentation

When Buying or Selling

Aside from the actual real estate contracts, there are many other forms that are utilized during the real estate process. However, the two discussed below are to be used without exception in both the buying and selling process throughout Canada. I've opted to do the explanations up front and just reference them later as they come up.

Agency Relationship - "Working with a REALTOR®"

Up until the mid-90's, a REALTOR® who worked with a buyer was actually a sub-agent of the seller. This meant that the buyer did not have representation. In practical terms, whatever the buyer disclosed to the REALTOR® was to be shared with the seller.

The real estate business has changed significantly since then. Before the consumer begins working with a REALTOR®, he should be aware of the kind of agency relationship he is entering. These are legal relationships with inherent duties. Establishing agency relationships is practiced throughout Canada.

When you and I first meet at my office, I generally ask you the kind of real estate experience you have had and if you are familiar with 'agency relationship'. At best, consumers are only vaguely familiar with the term. There are important legal implications so I like to give it a higher profile in my discussions. There is a small brochure entitled 'Working with a REALTOR®' which describes these relationships. I will give you an abbreviated and concise version of its contents.

What is Agency?

The *agency relationship* is between the principal (you) and the Brokerage (the real estate company). The REALTOR® who represents you is licensed under the Brokerage. The practical application is that I, as a licensed REALTOR® working under my Brokerage, have the authority to represent you in the real estate transaction when dealing with others.

When representing you, my fiduciary duties to you, under the Brokerage, are to look after your interests as if they were my own. This means: -

I have to disclose everything I know about the property and situation that may affect or influence your decision regarding the real estate transaction.

My duty includes protecting your negotiating position by not disclosing anything that would jeopardize it. I owe you undivided loyalty.

I must obey all your instructions as long as they are lawful.

I am not at liberty to disclose any of your confidences and must keep them confidential.

All my assigned duties must be exercised with reasonable care and skill.

I am accountable for all money and property that is placed with my Brokerage while acting on your behalf.

Dual Agency

Since, the agency relationship is between you and the Brokerage, it is possible for the property which interests you to be listed with the same Brokerage. In that instance, the Brokerage is representing both you and the seller and this then is known as dual agency.

Under these circumstances, the Brokerage cannot adhere to the original agency commitments towards both parties. This relationship will then have to be limited and both parties will have to agree to these limitations, in writing, prior to making an offer or receiving an offer.

Under *limited dual agency*, the limitations are as follows:-

The REALTORS®, *licensed under this Brokerage, will deal with buyers and sellers impartially. This means that they cannot help you negotiate price. They become facilitators of the transaction and not negotiators.*

REALTORS® *continue to have duties of disclosure except for three areas: No disclosures will be made regarding-*

> *Price and terms outside those contained within the offer*

> *The motivations to buy or sell*

> *Personal information unless it is part of the offer or if permission is received in writing.*

REALTORS® *must disclose all known physical defects of the property to the buyer.*

No Agency Relationship

There is also the option of using REALTOR® services *without having an agency relationship.* But even under these circumstances, the REALTOR® still has a legal and ethical commitment to you. This includes:-

Answering all your questions accurately and honestly

Explaining terms and forms used

Showing you properties

Preparing offer and counter-offers according to your direction

Presenting offers promptly

It does exclude disclosing anything relating to price and anything personal about the REALTOR'S® principal.

Signatures

Once 'agency' has been explained and is understood, you are asked to sign a form. You are only signing that this has been explained to you and that you may be signing additional documentation relating to agency later in the process.

The 'Working with a REALTOR®' brochure also discusses the collection and use of your personal information. Such information is required by cooperating participants of the real estate process. Your signature will also apply to your understanding regarding the collection of such private information.

Individual Identification Information Record

This form may also be referred to as FINTRAC - The Financial Transactions and Report Analysis Centre of Canada.

Anti-money laundering and terrorist financing legislation has been in existence as of 2001. Since that time, real estate agents have been required to report any cash transactions of $10,000 or more as well as suspicious real estate transactions. In addition, as of June 2008, the Federal Government of Canada instituted a new federal money laundering and anti-terrorist financing regulation. This new regulation requires that real estate agents, financial institutions and other professionals covered by this legislation identify customers who conduct financial transactions. This includes buying and selling real estate as well as depositing funds.

After explaining this legislation, I have you complete the required form which includes your full legal name, current address, date of birth and occupation. I must then view the original identification document. The type of document together with an identification number and issuing jurisdiction and expiry date must be recorded. This information is to be kept for 5 years.

If the consumer is a Corporation, the real estate agent must have Articles of Incorporation and Authorization for Signing Authority.

There are slight variations in this process depending on the circumstances but the collection of such information is mandatory.

Your REALTOR® - for Buyer

Vi Brown

Your REALTOR'S® Experience

If this were a book of fiction, you really wouldn't need to know much about me. But I felt compelled to write this book on real estate because, in my experience, consumers are not really aware of the full process. They come to my office and are truly puzzled about the procedures involved in purchasing a home or how to begin the process of selling their home.

Real estate continues to increase in paper work and complexity and I would like to provide, at least, a basic road map through the process of buying and selling. As a REALTOR® and your guide through this process, you should know some of my background and the kind of real estate I have practiced over nearly 20 years.

REALTORS® are diverse individuals as in any profession. We must adhere to our professional code and standards but are otherwise free to practice our craft.

Throughout my years in real estate, I have certainly made many observations and formulated some specific views. I have chosen to limit some real estate practices because they no longer seem relevant today. I'm getting ahead of myself and will save this till later.

Marketing Manager

My first career was as a marketing manager for a subsidiary of a multi-national corporation in the eastern part of Canada -- Quebec and Ontario. My position involved marketing, training, planning, forecasting, research, personnel, writing, committee work and much travel. After many years of a rewarding corporate career, it was time for a change.

Owner/Operator of Lodge

In my second career, I was self-employed somewhere in the wilderness. I had the opportunity to 'escape' to northern Ontario and become owner/operator of a fishing and hunting lodge with my husband. I abandoned my city life style and became a country woman.

I was literally living in the 'bush'. It was a 36 kilometre round trip to pick up my mail at the post office. There were no year-round residents except for us and another lodge owner further down the lake. However, there were many summer camps around the lake and it was a busy time during those months. The lake was about 17 miles long and about ½ mile wide at its widest. The lodge was near the center. The area had no delivery of any kind – no newspapers, pizza or mail. Nor was there any cable TV, no street lights or private telephone lines – just party lines. No paved roads and no sanding of winter roads except for some snow clearing. Winters were pretty isolated during the week but busy with ice fishing and snowmobiling on weekends.

The property consisted of rental cottages on the lake and a number of trailer sites for those who wanted to set them up for the summer. Of course, being on a gorgeous lake, we had boats and motors and gas service. The lodge housed a restaurant with a liquor license, small convenience store and our personal residence. We were open year-round and activities consisted of swimming, boating, fishing and wild life watching during the summer. Hunting grouse, deer and moose were the fall activities and in the winter there was ice fishing and snowmobiling. The amenities consisted of fresh air and very quiet nights, the haunting sound of loons, incredible northern light displays, the occasional bear, deer or moose on the property. In addition, we drank lake water, operated on a septic system, and had two TV channels in good weather.

Self-Proclaimed Real Estate Person

There is a time for everything but after many years of running this lodge, it was time to sell. The problem was that I couldn't find a real estate agent to market this property. The closest city with a real estate office was about 80 kilometres away. As far as I could determine, agents with this kind of experience were rare. I didn't want to list with someone who sold only city residential properties. I had no choice but

9

to try and sell this lodge myself. I proceeded with the advertising, the phone calls, answering questions and showing the property. This was a highly frustrating experience which took over a year. But, eventually the lodge sold.

My husband and I were quite used to this 'bush' lifestyle so we built a house about one kilometre up the lake from the lodge. Since we no longer had a business, I was looking for a new adventure and a new challenge.

REALTOR® - Ontario

Real estate sales – my third career! It seemed natural for me to sell recreational properties in the north. I knew all about hunting moose, deer and grouse and the license requirements and lotteries that had to be entered to get a desirable tag. Fishing the various species in the north, made me knowledgeable regarding open season dates and catch limits. As a restaurant operator, I was familiar with liquor laws, food handling regulations and health department requirements as well as the relevant taxation rules. I was a boater so could discuss boating regulations. As a snowmobiler, I knew all the connecting trails in many areas. Septic systems, drilled and shallow wells, the use of lake water as a drinking source were all familiar areas to me. I was aware of zoning by laws as well as the implication of living in unorganized townships.

After completing the real estate course, I specialized in such rural properties and businesses. I often travelled many kilometres to list properties. Sellers of these properties valued my knowledge and called on me. Aside from hunting and fishing resorts and cottages, this also evolved into the sale of motels, small hotels, restaurants, large resorts, hobby farms, acreages, waterfront properties and even some residential properties.

I did real estate by car, by boat and by snow machine. I wrote contracts in restaurants, in my car, on the hood of my car, on picnic tables, in boats and occasionally in a home. I was never close enough to my office.

When I first started out, I needed guidance to write contracts for such businesses. My office dealt primarily with residential properties and was not always able to adequately assist me. However, I was fortunate in knowing a very patient lawyer who helped me with appropriate clauses for contracts. These calls were often made from the field as I was drafting an offer. In those days, I had one of the very first cell phones, a rather large one to which I attached an extra long antennae so that I could get better reception. To this day, I am grateful that this lawyer always took my calls and provided the expertise I needed.

REALTOR® - British Columbia

As a result of a salmon fishing trip to British Columbia, my husband and I were so enthralled with BC's Vancouver Island that we moved here in 1996.

I had already challenged the BC real estate examination while in Ontario so was ready to begin my real estate career in BC when we arrived. This was going to be a bit different. I was going to be working in the city. No more jeans or boots or boats or snowmobiles. High heels – which I hadn't worn for many years—were going to be part of the dress code. I also had to get my jewellery out of moth balls. I was back to being a city woman.

Thankfully, the city was of reasonable size and it didn't take me forever to learn my way around. It helped that a colleague took me under her wing and showed me around. As we went on office tours together, she pointed out various landmarks that I should note. One day she also asked "Are directional signals optional in Ontario?" It seems that I had to increase my multi-tasking skills -- observing and signalling my turns!

For a REALTOR® going to a new city is, in effect, starting over -- no contacts, no history, no business. I did what any new REALTOR® did in those days – offer to do open houses, send out flyers, make phone calls and so on. Gradually, business came my way. My helpful colleague and I became involved in some real estate projects and found that we worked well together so we formed a business partnership. We dealt with residential properties and, because of my background, incorporated some rural and waterfront properties as well as businesses.

Managing Broker – BC

The partnership worked well. Business was good. After a few years, I became a co-owner of the real estate company as did my business partner. As a result of some changes in our company and further changes in management, our company required a new Broker. Given my management background and my real estate experience, my business partner suggested that I consider the position. After some discussions with the other co-owners, I agreed to become the Managing Broker. This required additional studies and a change of licensing after which I became qualified as a Broker. My new licensing also included the Property Management areas. I was a non-selling Broker and dealt full time with company business and REALTOR® activities.

I found that being a Broker was a very serious obligation. Brokers are responsible for all the real estate activities conducted by REALTORS® and by property management. If a REALTOR® incorrectly handles a real estate transaction and/or breeches the Code of Ethics and the Standards of Business Practice, the Broker is equally responsible whether the Broker was aware of the infraction or not. To this day, I have a high respect for Brokers taking on such commitments.

Real Estate Board – Director - BC

During my time as Managing Broker, I also became a Director at the local real estate board. It was an interesting insight into the workings of the board – the various committees – the functions of the Executive Officer and the board's relationship with the provincial Council.

The underlying theme in all this was to ensure that the consumer was well serviced by the real estate industry and well protected. The real estate boards are always prepared to answer consumer questions and to deal with complaints. It is their high priority to resolve such issues.

It was also a time when many internet suppliers were opening real estate websites. The Directors were exposed to many presentations illustrating how these internet websites would be of benefit to the REALTORS® if they listed their properties on these sites through the real estate board. There were many such sites in the making. After many discussions within the board and with other boards, it was concluded that the boards MLS® System was the best vehicle for REALTORS® and for consumers.

Over the years, the MLS® System has been updated and made more user friendly. Consumers can access listed properties on www.realtor.ca. It is the best consolidated list of properties available to the consumer. The MLS® System is financially maintained through fees charged to its licensed members – REALTORS® and real estate boards.

REALTOR® - BC

I have been a REALTOR® in two provinces and three cities. Victoria, BC is my current city. As with many self-employed professionals, a change of location means starting over and developing a new business base once again.

I have done commercial real estate over the years and am registered as a Commercial REALTOR® in Victoria. I now do selected commercial businesses and properties such as Bed & Breakfasts, RV Parks, equestrian properties, hobby farms, kennels, residential acreages and waterfront properties. Of course, residential properties are a large part of my work as well.

The company, I initially joined in Victoria, had several offices and often required an extra Broker to fill in during vacations and other absences. Consequently, my Broker's license remained active over the years.

More recently, I joined DFH Real Estate Ltd. and now work as an Associate Broker/REALTOR® - without Broker responsibilities - but fully engaged in real estate sales.

Buying a Home

The Beginning

You have decided to buy a home. Renting is no longer an option. You want to build some equity for the future. What can you afford? Small house? Condo? Where do you begin?

You have been living here for 25 years. You brought up your children in this home but now they are gone and have their own lives. This house is far too big for the two of you and it requires too much care. You are thinking of selling and buying a condo. Which should you do first - sell or buy? Where do you begin?

Your family is increasing. You need more space. What is your home worth? Can you afford a larger home? Where do you begin?

You are being transferred and have to find a home in a new city. Your company is allowing you several days for 'house shopping'. You will have to locate a REALTOR® to assist you. Will the REALTOR® accommodate you with the time you require? Where do you begin?

With the exception of a transfer, most consumers are able to look for a home on a more leisurely basis. As the thought of buying materializes, many consumers start browsing through real estate papers and other real estate publications. They may access the various internet sites including the MLS® System - www.realtor.ca - to see what properties are available in their neighbourhood of interest. Some may drive around favourite neighbourhoods to check out homes with for sale signs.

There are many ways to proceed but the most effective way is to find a REALTOR® that you are comfortable with and in whom you have confidence to represent you.

Consumer Concerns

Some consumers avoid contacting a REALTOR® because they are uncertain of what this entails.

Seeing All Listed Properties

I have had clients who asked me up front if I would show them other properties besides my own listings or the company's listings. The misconception is that REALTORS® don't wish to show other properties or that they don't have information on other companies' listings. The fact is that all REALTORS® have access to the information of properties listed on the MLS® System. REALTORS® often promote their properties to each other in the hope that one of them may have a suitable buyer for the property. REALTORS® are a cooperative group.

Availability of Information

Similarly, others only contact listing REALTORS® because they feel that REALTORS® from other companies may not have all the information and, specifically, may not have some helpful inside information that would assist the buyer. Personal information about the seller cannot be disclosed by the listing REALTOR® to a potential buyer or to any other REALTOR®. But, all property information must be shared.

Obtaining Addresses

Other consumers like to use the real estate paper and do their own drive-bys before they contact a REALTOR®. Often the address is not in the paper so they call the real estate office with the listing and ask for the address. If the MLS® number is in the ad, they can search it on www.realtor.ca and generally find the address. Because there are several days of lead time required to publish a paper, in a fast market some of these properties might already have pending offers. This is a very time consuming way to search for properties.

REALTOR® Fees

Another drawback for some consumers deals with their uncertainty of how a REALTOR® gets paid. This is easily clarified. In most instances, when I represent a buyer, my fee comes from the proceeds of the transaction. The listing REALTOR'S® Brokerage has a listing contract with the seller which specifies the dollar amount or the percentage of the selling price that the Brokerage will be paid upon the completion of the transaction. Out of that, it stipulates the dollar amount or percentage of the selling price that will be shared with the cooperating Brokerage - if different from the listing Brokerage.

The respective REALTORS® also have agreements with their Brokerages as to what percentages they will receive for their services. These agreements vary within a real estate company and among real estate companies. By the time the property is on the market, these contractual fees are already established, and, in most instances, are outside the buyer's sphere of influence.

'Pushy' REALTOR®

Consumer concerns wouldn't be complete without addressing 'pushy' REALTORS®. For the most part, this perception is generally due to the buyer and the REALTOR® working at different speeds. Some consumers only take a few moments to go through a home and decide whether it is on their potential list or not. Others scrutinize a property much more carefully before coming to such a decision. Some buyers spend a great deal of time evaluating their choices before making an offer. For others, it is a straight forward decision.

REALTORS® have to adjust to the pace of their clients and, generally, do. A little communication usually clears up the problem. REALTORS® are there to facilitate the process by ensuring that you, as buyers, have all the information necessary to make informed decisions -- at your pace.

The 'Door Opener'

There are times that I receive a call from a consumer who wishes to see a property. I don't normally respond to such a request but ask the potential buyers to first come to my office to discuss their requirements. Often they do and occasionally they don't.

In the past, I responded to such requests but soon learned from them. The following is an example of what transpired on one occasion.

The caller wanted to see a property later that same day. I agreed to this instead of suggesting that we should first meet. It was my listing, close to my office and it was vacant. I asked the caller some important questions: "Are you working with a REALTOR®?" The answer was "No" and so I felt I was not infringing on another REALTOR® or wasting my time.

There are occasions when a consumer calls on several REALTORS® to view properties. If that is the case, it is only the REALTOR® who eventually writes the offer who is not wasting his time. All those who show homes that are not of interest are simply 'Door Openers'. They are wasting their time and really have no recourse because they know nothing about the buyer's wants or needs.

Another question: "Have you been pre-qualified for a mortgage?" "Yes, up to $500,000." A good answer since it attests to the seriousness of the buyer. So, I agreed to meet Joyce, this potential buyer, at the vacant house at 4:30 p.m.

I arrived a few minutes ahead of time to open the house and put on the lights. Shortly, a gentleman came by but I wasn't sure why he was there. I was expecting a female. I soon found out, that this was apparently a relative of the potential buyer who might co-sign for the mortgage and was, therefore, previewing the home.

At this point, I was somewhat uneasy as I knew nothing about this person or the person who actually made the call. Nor did I notify anyone in my office that I was showing a property. As he viewed this house, I allowed the gentlemen to browse through this vacant home on his own as I stayed close to the open front door with my cell phone in hand with the emergency number on speed dial. When he was finished, he simply thanked me and returned to his car. He had no questions nor was I prepared to address anything either. I was simply glad that he left.

I didn't know how serious these buyers were or what their timing might have been. They obviously didn't want a REALTOR®. They wanted a 'Door Opener'! In not having buyers first come to my office where I could have obtained information about them and their housing needs, I not only wasted my time but could also have unnecessarily exposed myself to danger.

Meeting with the REALTOR®

Now when I get a phone call from you, the consumer, indicating that you plan on making a real estate purchase, I ask you to come to my office. This is a serious purchase and it requires setting up some important ground work.

From your point of view, you should know all the aspects that make up the buying process. This also includes gathering all available information so that you can make the best decisions.

From my point of view, as your REALTOR®, I would like to know details about your real estate needs and wants, your timing and whether you have been pre-approved for a mortgage.

I generally begin by obtaining your legal names (essential for contracts), address, home phone number, work numbers, cell numbers, fax numbers and email addresses.

Usually, I provide you with some highlights about my real estate company and my professional background. I then want to know about you so may ask you some general questions about yourself-- perhaps your work or other places you have lived. At this point, this is not a fact gathering session but an opportunity to build some rapport. I find that a little personal information enhances a work relationship.

I then proceed to the kind of home you are looking for -- house, condo, townhouse or mobile --what size, how many bedrooms, bathrooms, garage, yard requirements and location. I have an outline of my questions and make notes as we go along. I enquire as to whether or not you have been pre-qualified for a mortgage and whether or not you have a down payment. I also ask you about timing -- when you wish to be in your new home.

In discussing all these elements, we develop a sense of how we would work together. I actually address that point and make sure that you are comfortable with me and feel that I have a good grasp of what you are looking for in a home. I then proceed.

Agency Relationship - 'Working with a REALTOR®' Brochure

After establishing the kind of home you are looking for, I begin with some of the paperwork. I explain the agency relationship to you at this point and have you sign the form. This has been described at the outset of the book so I will not elaborate further here.

Exclusive Buyer Agency Contract

Next is the Exclusive Buyer Agency Contract. I highlight the key clauses of this contract. Essentially, it is a commitment between the Brokerage, represented by me, the REALTOR®, and you, the buyer-- similar in intent to the Listing Contract signed by sellers.

Since we will be investing time in each other, this contract commits us to each other for a specific period of time. Such loyalty creates a positive and productive relationship.

I will be making you aware of all listed properties in your areas of interest and acting as your agent working on your behalf. If a property is for sale but not listed on the board's MLS® System, I, representing my Brokerage, can enter into a fee agreement with the seller without acting as an agent for the seller but still working on your behalf.

You as the buyer, agree to use my REALTOR® services exclusively for the agreed upon time period and provide me with sufficient information so that I can act in an informed manner on your behalf.

This contract also provides the buyer's Brokerage with a guaranteed fee which is then stipulated in the contract. Fees vary from REALTOR® to REALTOR® and from Brokerage to Brokerage. It is against the Competition Act to have fixed fees. So I would set the fee that my Brokerage would receive through this contract.

When you, the buyer, select a home that you wish to purchase, I will advise you what fee is offered, if any. If it is less than stipulated in the contract, you will pay my Brokerage the shortfall plus applicable taxes or, I can, with your permission, see if I can obtain my stipulated fee through the other Brokerage or via a fee agreement. You also have the option of by-passing that home and selecting another.

To put this in perspective, when such a situation arises, my fee has generally been met by the listing Brokerages or I have been able to negotiate my fee through a fee agreement.

Once you understand and agree with the terms of the Exclusive Buyer Agency Contract, and we have signed the contract, you are no longer simply a consumer or customer but become my client. As such, this gives me the authority to represent you and legally obligates me to look after your interests. It does NOT give me the authority to sign on your behalf - such authority would have to be provided in writing.

It should be noted, that a buyer agency relationship can also be implied by the conduct of the parties and does not necessarily require a signed document.

I then move on to the next piece of paperwork.

Individual Identification Information Record

This identification form is also referred to as FINTRAC - The Financial Transactions and Report Analysis Centre of Canada. I explain it to you and have you complete the form. This too has been described in the earlier part of this book.

Mortgage Pre-Approval

Now that I have established the kind of home you would like and we have dispensed with the initial paperwork, my focus is on price range. To establish the price range, you need to be pre-approved for a mortgage.

If you have been truly pre-approved, that means that you have provided your financial institution or a mortgage broker with your employment history, pay stubs, tax assessments, any credit card debt and other financial obligations. In turn, the lender has assessed all this information, did a credit check and you have received a letter, from your financial institution or mortgage broker, stipulating the amount of mortgage for which you qualify. The net result of being pre-approved is that the only missing ingredient in this process is the actual home. Once you have selected the home, the mortgage process can proceed.

However, if you have gone to a financial institution or mortgage broker, and you have not provided any of your personal financial data but simply talked about it, then you probably do not have anything in writing. Any verbal price range that has been given to you is at best tentative and cannot be relied upon. There is always a chance that some financial element has been overlooked or not all debts have been incorporated. There also may be other factors such as job stability, past bankruptcy or credit history that has not been addressed and could have mortgage implications. To avoid disappointment, I would suggest that you go back to your financial institution or mortgage broker and obtain proper mortgage pre-approval.

I have included a chapter entitled 'Financing Options' that will provide you with some factors you will need to consider when 'shopping' for a mortgage.

Internet Search

Now that we have examined some of the financial factors you may encounter, we are finally ready to check the MLS® System for appropriate properties.

Many real estate boards have specific programmes for REALTORS® that enables them to do detailed searches and also enables the REALTOR® to actually email such results to their clients. Some programmes are quite elaborate whereby the client, having received listings fitting his criteria, can mark his 'favourites', or 'possibilities' or place them in a 'discard' category if they are not of interest. Then, on a daily basis, if properties come on to the market place meeting his criteria, they are emailed to him. In this way the client continues to stay up to date with new entries.

I now know the kind of home you are seeking so I input some specific criteria, including an approximate price range, and do a search. A fair number of properties come up but I don't wish to fine tune the criteria any further because, at this point, it is in your best interest to see a broader spectrum of properties from which to choose the ones you wish to view.

I do two things with this search. First, I email it to you so that when at home, you can browse through and categorize them and or delete the ones that are not of interest. I also print out the search.

Concluding First REALTOR® Meeting

At this point, you have been with me for about an hour and probably are in information overload! There is still more information to share but this is a good place to stop for now.

I have a 'Buyer's Information Package' for you. It covers some aspects of what we discussed and also has new material. The package contains a copy of the 'Contract of Purchase and Sale' and Addendums that you will encounter when you have found the right home. It is a good idea to become familiar with these documents.

I also provide you with copies of all the documents you have signed.

If you have not been pre-approved for a mortgage, it is best to schedule an appointment so that we can verify the price range and avoid any disappointments at a later time.

You also have a broad selection of properties that you can review. You may wish to do some drive-bys and/or select some you wish to see. Once you have made your choices, let me know and I will set up the appointments so that we can start the selection process.

Making Appointments for Showings

Once you have selected the properties you wish to see and call me, I then arrange for the appointments. Depending on local customs and/or arrangements the listing REALTOR® may have made with his seller, I either call the listing REALTOR® or the seller to arrange an appointment to show the property. There is usually a window of approximately two hours to attend the property during which time the seller is gone. Potential buyers are much more comfortable viewing homes when the owners are absent.

I have worked in cities where the use of lock boxes was not the norm so this meant picking up keys from real estate offices -- a much longer process. But in many areas, lock boxes are used and this makes the showing process far more convenient.

In order to be able to work within the required time frames, I have to plan my route in a logical fashion and also anticipate how long my clients will take to look through a home.

If the properties are within adjacent municipalities, I may be able to show between 6-8 homes if they are on lock boxes. I usually verify to see if my client is comfortable with that range. When I have an out of town buyer who has time constraints, I have often shown double this number of homes. This requires an early start and late finish with lunch on the run!

If my clients consist of 1 or 2 people, I prefer to take them in my car so that I can get some feedback on what they have seen -- what they like and dislike. This helps me to better understand the kind of home that might be suitable. Otherwise, they simply follow me in their own vehicle since meaningful discussions become difficult in a group setting.

'Shopping'

On the appointed day, you meet me at my office and I hand you a clip board and pen as well as a 'tour' sheet of properties where you can record key elements of the properties you see to help you remember them later. I have already programmed my GPS with all the addresses for the quickest routes from one property to the next and we are ready to 'go shopping'!

When you first start to view homes, you have a vision of the new home in mind. In fact, you have described it to me at our first meeting. Most of the time, one single home does not have all these desirable elements. As you view one home after another, your vision begins to change and the focus becomes more realistic. By the end of one day's viewing, you have gathered some good insight into what is important for you to have in a home.

I generally suggest that you do 'plus and minus' list for each home you have seen. This helps you sort out which home you may wish to see again and helps you to select other homes to view. I also check to see if any other properties have come onto the market place in the past couple of days that we need to put on our 'shopping list'.

If during the first day's viewings, a home doesn't rise to the top of your list, I suggest that you select others you would like to see and give me a call so I can set up further appointments.

It takes perhaps 2 or 3 outings before a client is ready to select one on which to make an offer. Frequently the home that is selected was viewed on the first day. But viewing others simply confirms that the first choice is the best choice. As a REALTOR®, I have to respect my client's decision making process and timing. In most instances, this is all within the framework of reasonableness. Extreme unreasonableness is rare but has to be addressed and resolved.

It is worth noting that in a fast market where many buyers are competing for the available properties, sometimes you don't have the luxury of time. In those instances, I have warned my clients that if they have found a home they really like, they should seriously consider placing an offer immediately. That really sounds like a 'pushy' REALTOR®!

Nevertheless, it had to be said. Some wanted the extra time to discuss the property over the course of the evening and then decided to make an offer the next morning. Unfortunately, the property had sold the previous evening. The search then continued and the mind set adjusted to the circumstances.

The Offer

After all the viewings and evaluations, you have made your selection and are now prepared to make an offer. You have already looked over the blank Contract of Purchase and Sale and the Addendums that I included in your Buyer's Package. I will now go over the major parts -- primarily the parts that have to be completed.

Price

To help you decide the price you will offer, I provide you with all the information available to that point. I obtain the Property Assessment for this property, the listing history as well as current and more recently sold similar properties in the area. This will enable you to evaluate the asking price of this home and determine if the price is within a normal range of similar properties in the area you are purchasing.

I am happy to participate in the discussion and lend my experience to the situation but ultimately, the price offered is your decision.

Property Assessment

I answer any questions you may have as you deliberate. One of the questions is generally about the dollar value of the property on the assessment. An assessment is not the same as an appraisal. Assessments are used as a base for property taxes.

In BC, property assessments reflect prices as of July 1 of the previous year. In addition, year-to-year adjustments are based on a formula and not by inspections. For these reasons, assessments do not reflect market value today.

Not all regions utilize the previous year's information. Ontario, for instance, uses the same base year for four consecutive years. This certainly increases the distance between assessed value and market value.

Property Appraisal

A property appraisal can be done any time by inspecting the property. For residential properties, the direct comparison approach of similar properties is utilized. The appraised value reflects market value on that day. An appraisal loses accuracy and validity over time because of market changes.

Deposit

I recommend that a respectable deposit be included to demonstrate the seriousness of your offer. The deposit forms part of the selling price and is generally returned to the buyer if a satisfactory agreement cannot be reached. The usual process for releasing the deposit and the contract is through the signing of a release by both seller and buyer.

The deposit is usually held by the real estate company as a stakeholder and not for the benefit of either the buyer or seller. In many jurisdictions deposits are required by certified cheque or bank draft.

In some areas, the custom is not to take a deposit until all conditions have been removed. This is not my preference. It has been my experience that sellers look much more favourably at an offer with a deposit, and even more favourably when it is a generous deposit. When I am representing my client, I want to ensure that his offer is seen in the best possible light. A good deposit accomplishes this.

Contract Dates

I then cover all the dates that appear in the contract.

Of course, there is the date you write the **offer**. Then we discuss the date you would like to have the keys to actually move into your new home - the **possession** date. Once we establish that, we can establish the day that money and title change hands or **completion** date. This day is usually a day or two before possession date. Some jurisdictions also have an **adjustment** date which can be the same as completion date. This refers to any financial adjustments the lawyer or notary may have to make with respect to property taxes, prepaid fees, rents and the like.

The offer has a limited life span. This means that it is only open for acceptance for a specified period of time. This can be as little as a couple of hours or a couple of days or even more depending on the market conditions and situation. In some jurisdictions, this date is referred to as the **irrevocable** date.

The last date in this grouping is the **acceptance** date. This is the date on which both buyer and seller agree to the terms of this contract. This may be the same as the offer date or several days later if counter-offers have gone back and forth. Besides the acceptance date itself, often the time of acceptance is also noted.

Agency Relationship

The Contract of Purchase and Sale also addresses this relationship. It requires that we stipulate who represents the buyer; who represents the seller; is it dual agency; or is one of the parties not represented.

We discussed all of these scenarios when you signed the `Working with a REALTOR®` brochure at our first meeting. The contract requires that the relationships be spelled out here.

Terms Agreeable to both Buyer and Seller

Clients often ask me what kind of subject to's or conditions should be placed in a contract. There are major conditions that have to be inserted to protect you but aside from that, there are few restrictions. The important aspect is that both buyer and seller have to agree to the terms.

Perhaps this example will illustrate my point.

I had clients who had been renting for years and had been thinking of purchasing a small home. Prices were too high for a single family home but a mobile home might be possible. They drove through some mobile home parks and found one that they just loved - on a hill with ocean view and a sun room! They called me and I suggested that they get pre-approved. A few days later, they told me that they couldn't get financing for a mobile. I then recommended that they see someone else and I arranged the appointment. In another few days, they called and said that they could get pre-approved, if they had an additional $3,000 for their down payment. Also the pre-approval dollar amount was a bit less than the asking price for the mobile. They indicated that they had a relatively new scooter that they have been trying to sell and if they could sell it they would have enough money for the down payment.

To disclose any of my client's personal information, I needed to obtain their permission. Having obtained it, I verified their situation with the mortgage broker and then called the listing REALTOR®. I chose to discuss part of the circumstances with the REALTOR® instead of proceeding with an offer because this was a unique situation and I didn't wish to waste any one's time. I explained that I had a client who was very interested in her mobile home listing but was a little short on a down payment and could not meet the full price. However, with a little creativity and flexibility we might be able to work it out.

The REALTOR® approached her client and briefed him on the circumstances and, although not excited at the prospect, he was anxious to see an offer. So, after my clients viewed this mobile home, I drew up the offer.

The price was the maximum they could be approved for and, among other conditions, the contract was subject to the seller taking on the scooter by completion day in exchange for $3,000. The seller accepted the contract as written. Apparently, the seller was anxious to relocate and purchasing the scooter was a means by which he was able to move on with his life. Needless to say, I had very happy clients who delighted in their new home!

It has been my experience that a little creativity and working 'outside the box' can turn into a win-win situation for buyer and seller. Those times make my job so delightful!

Inclusions in the Purchase

As a rule, all fixtures are included in a purchase. These generally pertain to items which are 'attached'-- light fixtures, doors, curtain rods, tracks and valances, fixed carpeting and so on. Not everyone views 'fixtures' in the same way so it is best to specify some of these inclusions. For example, a built in vacuum cleaner is attached and should, therefore, be included. However, the attachments may not be included!

Items like washer and dryer and stove and fridge are not automatically included unless they are built in. Items such as drapes and curtains are not automatically included but the rods are. When in doubt - clarify!

Subject to Clauses or Conditions

All subjects/conditions must be clearly written, have a time frame for satisfying the condition and indicate if they benefit the buyer or seller or both.

Financing

We now decide what conditions are required to protect you in this contract. As your REALTOR®, I certainly have recommendations in this area. The major one is the financing. If I don't include this condition, and for some reason your mortgage does not materialize, you are still committed to this contract. Even if you have been pre-approved, I still include this clause because the property forms part of the mortgage qualification.

Home Inspection

Another major subject to clause deals with the condition of the home you are about to purchase. To make certain that you are purchasing a sound home, this offer will be conditional on having a home inspection.

We have gone through the home and made some observations but we have not examined it for structural soundness nor have we seen the roof and possibly other crucial areas. I recommend that you hire a home inspector to check this home. A few hundred dollars can avoid a lot of problems. A home inspection is a worthwhile investment. If for some reason you choose not to have a home inspection, I note, in the contract, that you have declined to have one. I want to be absolutely certain that you have understood the danger of skipping this step.

A chapter entitled 'Your Home Inspector' - written by Robert Hughes will provide you with more information about home inspections.

Property Title

You must ensure that the title to this property is in good order and so we make this a condition of the contract. There are often non-financial charges that run with the land that you should understand and need to accept.

The 'Your Lawyer' chapter written by Kelly Orr will go into some of these elements.

Fire/Property Insurance

When you obtain a mortgage, the lender requires that you have your home insured. Some of the considerations for the insurer are heating, plumbing, electrical and so on. Through a home inspection, your professional home inspector can provide you with much of this kind of information.

It is wise to make this a condition of the contract. You don't need to get the insurance at this time but you need to verify that you will be able to have the home insured. No insurance -- no mortgage.

From an insurance company's perspective, if a property has had a great deal of claims, they may choose to no longer insure the property once the policy expires or is cancelled. This is another good reason to make certain that insurance can be obtained.

Property Disclosure

It is a common practice, when a seller lists his property, to complete a Property Disclosure statement. The form includes a variety of factors about the property which the seller must answer honestly to the best of his knowledge. This does not, however, excuse you, the buyer, from making your own inquiries. The Property Disclosure is subject to the buyer's approval and forms part of the contract.

Other Considerations

It is impossible to incorporate every possible situation in discussing the real estate process in these pages. No real estate transaction is exactly the same as another. The conditions above are almost always incorporated in a contract.

If the home is a condo or townhouse, there are additional clauses pertaining to strata minutes and other documents that are also incorporated.

If the home is a mobile, clauses pertaining to obtaining rules and regulations and management approval are often included. There could be a number of other situations that could warrant a subject to clause but they can't all be covered here. But this will certainly alert you about other possible concerns.

Aside from subject to's or conditions, sometimes we include statements that we wish the seller to acknowledge. These statements are not conditions that would impact the contract but areas that the buyer seeks agreement. For example, if the seller has begun a project such as painting a room or fixing flooring in a room, often the buyer would appreciate the completion of such a project and such a statement may be included in the offer.

I like to minimize the inclusions of such statements as much as possible because I don't want the seller to be distracted with so many items that he loses the essence of the offer.

This is for the benefit of the buyer - my client. It is my obligation to include whatever my buyer wishes but it is also my duty to give him the benefit of my experience and then he can make the decision as to what he wishes to include.

On one occasion, I actually suggested that my buyers include a particular statement.

We had viewed this country home twice. The property had an accessory building that could be used as a small barn or large garage. In the corner of this building was a stable which housed, not a horse, but a beautiful black lab and her new puppies. It seemed as if my clients spent more time looking at the puppies than the house.

When we were almost finished writing the offer, which I considered to be a good offer, I asked them if they wanted me to include a puppy in the offer. They couldn't believe that I could do that! I could and I did. My clients got the property they dreamed of and an unexpected bonus -- a black lab puppy to call their own.

Setting up Appointment to Present Offer

Once the offer is completed and signed I make a call to the listing REALTOR® indicating that I have an offer on the property and schedule an appointment to present it. I do not usually disclose anything about the offer to the other REALTOR® over the telephone.

Although in many regions it has become the custom to simply fax the offer to the listing agent, it has always been my preference to present the offer myself. By presenting the offer, I feel there is a better opportunity to come to a consensus. Of course, there are times when this is not possible -- for example, when the seller is out of town.

I also ask you to keep yourself available so that I can contact you regarding the status of the offer.

Presenting Offer

The custom is generally to meet at the REALTOR'S® office or the sellers' home. Present at this meeting are the sellers, their REALTOR® and I. I mentally select those things that I will disclose to the sellers about my buyers and seek permission from my clients to do so.

Sellers like to hear a little about who is making an offer on their home and I like to oblige by satisfying some of that interest. It tends to create a more cooperative environment. I then give a copy of the offer to the listing REALTOR® and I continue with the presentation of the offer. I make certain that I advise the group that I have a deposit in the form of a certified cheque and point to it in my folder.

I conclude by asking the group if they have any questions. Often there are questions such as "How important are the dates to your client?" or "Are your clients pre-approved for their mortgage?" It is useful to respond to such questions because it facilitates the process of buyer and seller agreeing to terms. It should be noted, that I am very cautious in such conversations. I don't disclose anything about my clients that would compromise their negotiating position.

After the listing REALTOR® is satisfied that he has all the information necessary, he asks me to leave so that he and his clients can discuss the offer privately. If the REALTOR® feels that he can deal with the offer in a short amount of time, he may ask me to wait in my car. Otherwise, I will go back to my office and wait to hear from him. This, of course, also depends on how long the offer is open. If it is open for a brief time, I am more likely to wait in my car. If, however, it is open a day or so, I will go on with my business and wait for a call from the REALTOR®. I will also call you and give you an update.

Sometimes, an offer is accepted as written. This is more likely when it is a 'clean' offer -- not complicated with unusual clauses, has reasonable time frames and the price offered is deemed reasonable. Counter-offers, however, are the norm.

I always remind you, the buyer, that you have three choices when you receive a counter-offer. You can accept it, reject it or counter back. But, any time you make a change to the contract, it is like a new contract. The other party has the same choices. It is important to keep that in mind when negotiating. I work in your best interests and explain your options and their consequences but you are the decision maker.

Accepted Offer

Now that we have an accepted offer, you meet me at my office and we continue the process. By this time, the listing REALTOR® has provided all the related paperwork pertaining to the property such as -- title, Property Disclosure statement and survey certificate, if available. This is not an inclusive list and may vary depending on the kind of property you are purchasing.

You carefully review the Property Disclosure statement that the seller has completed. If you have any questions about it, I contact the REALTOR® for clarification. If you are then satisfied with it, I ask you to sign and date it and it becomes part of the contract.

I also have you review the title documents and suggest that any questions should be directed to your lawyer for clarification.

You receive copies of all the related property paperwork and copies of the accepted offer for your records. I fax a copy of the completed offer and a print out of the MLS® listing to your financial institution indicating that we require approval prior to the written subject due date and request that approval be sent in writing via fax.

Generally, I utilize only one date for all the conditions because it simplifies matters. However, the conditions have to be removed in a logical manner. For instance, a home inspection costs several hundred dollars so I don't want you to spend that money until we can confirm that your mortgage has been approved. Hence, my request that mortgage approval take place 2-3 days before the stipulated date in the offer.

During this period, you should also make inquiries about home insurance to satisfy yourself that this will not be an issue.

At this point, I ask you which lawyer or notary you will be using so that my office can send the documents to his/her office. I suggest that you call your legal representative to advise him that you have purchased a home and that the documents will be sent by the real estate company representing you. I then process my paperwork and certified deposit cheque to set things in motion.

Congratulations are in order for having completed a major part of your buying process!

Removing Subjects/Conditions

Financing

The primary focus is to have the financing condition satisfied. All documents have been submitted together with all information so the lender now obtains an appraisal.

Arrangements were made and the next day, I received a fax indicating that financing had been approved.

Home Inspection

The next major condition for removal is the home inspection. My clients selected an inspector from a list I provided and scheduled a time that was convenient for all concerned. One of the customs is for the selling REALTOR® to provide access to the home inspector and to be there for the walk through with the buyers. I have two choices. I can stay while the home inspector does his work and busy myself with some paperwork or I can leave and return for the walk through.

If I am not present during the entire inspection, I leave instructions for the home inspector not to allow any one access until I return, including my clients. It is not the responsibility of the home inspector to either allow any one else access or to supervise others who come before the scheduled time. His responsibility is to do the home inspection in a timely and thorough manner. The seller's expectation is that the REALTOR® will be present and I feel that this has to be honoured.

You are ready to hear the results of the inspection. You meet me at the home at the scheduled time and the home inspector shares his findings and provides you with a written report. Except for normal wear, no significant issues were found. You are satisfied and will remove the condition.

Property Title

You are satisfied with the title after discussing it with your lawyer.

Property Disclosure

You have already reviewed and signed the Property Disclosure.

Fire/Property Insurance

You have contacted a home insurance company and provided them with the information they require and will be obtaining coverage.

Disclosure of Remuneration

One more piece of paperwork is required in some jurisdictions. British Columbia calls it 'Disclosure of Remuneration' whereby the selling brokerage declares what fees or rewards it will receive, directly or indirectly and from whom.

Such a disclosure enables the buyer to see if the brokerage / REALTOR® has any vested interest in the transaction.

Processing Paperwork

It is now time to remove all the subjects/conditions.

I have drawn up the appropriate amendment. Since all these conditions were for the buyer's benefit, only you are required to sign it.

A copy of this document will be distributed - to you - the financial institution - my office who will send to your lawyer and a copy to the listing REALTOR®.

The paperwork is concluded and finalized. It is now time to start packing.

I will contact you a day or two before possession date to set up a time and give you the keys to your home. In the meantime, call me if I can be of further help.

Congratulations!

More about Financing Options

Vi Brown

Obtaining Financing

At this point, it may be useful to discuss some of the factors you should take into account when looking for financing. You want to be sure that you have made a selection that is in your best interest.

Most people talk to their bank when they are thinking of making a purchase. They go to their branch and discuss mortgages. Sometimes they may get information on interest rates and perhaps a price range based on some cursory information or they may be asked to return with certain documentation pertaining to income, assets and debts so that the buyer can obtain pre-approval.

I addressed this issue earlier but it is worth repeating. If you have not brought in your documentation pertaining to income, assets and debts, you probably have not been pre-approved! You may have been given a dollar figure up to a certain amount but don't rely on it. The homework has not been done.

A pre-approval means that the financial institution has your entire financial history and has done a credit check. At that point, you may have discussed interest rates and the bank has offered to lock in a current rate for 90 days. The time line varies from bank to bank.

Going to your bank is a good thing. However, shop around for your interest rate. Even if you have been a long time customer at your bank, they won't necessarily give you their best rate unless you ask. Call other banks or call a mortgage broker and have the broker shop around for you.

If you want to be inspired to shop around, do a little math and find out what it would cost you to carry a mortgage over a 25 year period at various interest rates. This may also inspire you to increase your payments.

Remember to 'shop' around -- it could save you lots of money!!

Some Mortgage Terms

The financing world has a specific terminology that you may not be familiar with particularly if you are a first time buyer. Here are a few that you may run into:

Mortgage - This is actually a two-part document - one specifies the details of that specific mortgage and the second part deals with the standard mortgage obligations

Mortgagor - the borrower, the buyer

Mortgagee - the lender

Guarantor - There are times when a financial institution will only lend funds if there is someone who will guarantee payment if the mortgagor defaults

Amortization Period - the length of time it would take to repay the mortgage - often it is 25-35 years

Term - This refers to the length of the current mortgage agreement which can be anywhere from 6 months to 10 years. When the term expires, it can be renewed subject to a new term and new interest rate or it can be paid out. Many moons ago, the amortization period was also the term period. However, with changing interest rates, lenders do not wish to lock in for that length of time so the process has been broken into smaller increments or terms.

Interest Rate - The interest rate is the cost of borrowing and dictates your monthly payments. Part of your payment is principal (the borrowed amount) and the other part is the interest (the cost of borrowing). The interest rate not only affects your monthly payments but also how much you can borrow -- the lower the rate - the smaller your payments - the more you can borrow.

Closed Mortgage - This means that you cannot make any changes. It may or may not limit you in making extra payments, such as on anniversary dates of the mortgage. It may prevent portability and you will certainly incur a penalty if you were to terminate such a mortgage.

However, it does provide stability in that you know exactly what your payments will be for the term.

Open Mortgage - This kind of mortgage can be paid off at any time prior to maturity without any penalty. It is not a favourite of lenders and often the interest rate is higher.

Fixed Interest Rate - During the term of the mortgage, the rate remains the same.

Variable Interest Rate - Such an interest rate fluctuates with the market and can change from month to month. If you opt for the variable, you have to keep track of the market trends.

Conventional Mortgage - To obtain such a mortgage, most financial institutions require a larger down payment usually 20-25%. If you have such a down payment, you can save yourself a few dollars by not requiring mortgage insurance and avoiding charges from corporations such as CMHC (Canadian Mortgage and Housing).

Mortgage Insurance - This is not the same as mortgage life insurance which pays your mortgage at the time of your death. Mortgage insurance protects the lender should you default on your payments. If you do not have a conventional mortgage, the lender will obtain mortgage insurance and pass the cost on to you. The cost is a percentage of your mortgage - the smaller your down payment the higher the cost for mortgage insurance. This cost is often added to your mortgage.

CHMC Insured Mortgage - As above, if you do not have sufficient down payment to be classified as a conventional mortgage, you will have to pay for mortgage insurance provided by CHMC. There are also other companies competing with CMHC and may have different criteria. Your bank or mortgage broker can inform you further.

Gross Debt Service (GDS) - This refers to your total housing costs which may include principal, interest, taxes, heat and 1/2 of any strata fees. This tends to run up to 32% of total income. The rate can vary a bit.

<u>Total Debt Service</u> - This is a key factor dictating your eligibility for a mortgage! The financial institutions will use your income and then calculate all your debts - your housing costs (GDS) and then add any other loans you have such as credit card debt, car payments and so on. The percentage is in the neighbourhood of up to 40% of your total income - there may be a slight variance depending on the financial institution.

<u>Portability</u> - If you have a portable mortgage that means that you can transfer your mortgage to a new home often subject to an appraisal and an updated credit check. There may also be a time frame for transferring the mortgage so ask about that. A portable mortgage can be a great advantage if your original mortgage rate is lower than the current rate.

Mortgage Options

There are two major factors which can influence your choice of mortgage options -- circumstances and interest rates. Let me briefly address some of the options available.

Obtaining Mortgage through a Mortgage Broker

There are numerous mortgage brokers. Generally, they are not affiliated with a bank but have access to many lenders including banks. They can 'shop' around for the best rates for you and a mortgage package that meets your needs and criteria. They can also select a mortgage insurer that may fit your criteria better.

Lenders differ in their financial criteria. For example, lenders often differ regarding the self-employed, those who have gone bankrupt, those who have had other debt issues, those who have sporadic employment records, those who are non-residents and so on. An experienced mortgage broker can often find the right fit and the best interest rate for the circumstances. As a rule, you can get a better rate through a mortgage broker than you would get at a bank.

Mortgage brokers are highly motivated to do their best to obtain a mortgage for you. They are not salaried so their pay day only comes when they arrange a mortgage for you.

This does not cost you. Mortgage brokers that obtain residential mortgages are generally paid by the lender.

Mortgage brokers often indicate that they have numerous lenders, 40 and more. That is not to say that they consult each of these for a mortgage. An experienced mortgage broker knows which lenders to approach depending on the circumstances of the buyer.

Mortgage brokers may be limited in some of the other financing options which may be better addressed by banks.

Obtaining Mortgage through a Bank

Although banks can handle a number of financing options, they do not always address every financial circumstance of a buyer. They have their 'products' that they promote and it may not necessarily be a fit for that particular buyer.

The branch loans people often have different levels of experience and may miss an opportunity to provide a mortgage. I have sent such a buyer to a mortgage broker where he obtained a mortgage. In some instances, this is due to lack of experience or lack of incentive to research further since there is always a guaranteed pay day.

As I previously noted, you have to be sure to ask for the best rate and not accept the bank's posted rate. If you wish to deal with your own bank, you may even have to inform them of the better rate you can get elsewhere.

Aside from going to the bank's branch, many banks have their mobile mortgage brokers. They are usually much more experienced and often have access to other lenders. This varies with the bank so you have to ask the right questions. These mobile mortgage brokers are probably a better option than your branch staff in terms of accessibility, experience and options. They may also be better equipped to handle other financing options such as bridge loans, equity loans and refinancing.

Obtaining a Mortgage through a Credit Union

This is also a viable option if you deal with a credit union. You usually have to be or become a member. Again, make certain that you have inquired elsewhere regarding interest rates to insure that you are getting the best rate.

Whereas, some banks are reluctant to finance mobile homes, many credit unions do so. With the high cost of housing in some areas, mobile homes are a good option for many.

Assuming Seller's Mortgage

When interest rates are on the rise and the seller has a mortgage at a rate lower than the current rate, the buyer can benefit. It is a good selling point for the seller and a financial opportunity for the buyer.

Sometimes buyers assume that they can just take over the mortgage without going through the qualification process but that is not the case. A buyer has to qualify in the same fashion as if it were a new mortgage. The advantage is the low interest rate.

The seller's mortgage may be less than the buyer requires. This can be accommodated in several ways, one of them being to top it up to the necessary amount and offer a blended rate which would still be a savings for the buyer.

This could be a good option for the buyer and should not be overlooked.

Seller Take Back Mortgage

There are times when a seller has equity in the property which he would like to invest. Real estate has proven to be a good investment choice. If this is the avenue that the seller wishes to pursue, he will often make it known in the listing.

Although the seller will certainly want to do a credit check and have a down payment, there may be greater flexibility in the payment plan. For instance, a seller take back mortgage is generally open and can be paid out without penalty. The interest rate may also be somewhat lower than an open mortgage at a financial institution.

It is certainly a worthwhile option to explore if it presents itself.

Equity Line of Credit

If your plan is to purchase a second property, there are numerous plans by which you can use the equity in your current home to finance the new property instead of acquiring a conventional mortgage on the second property. Generally, you can borrow as much as you require up to a specific limit that the financial institution sets. There are also various repayment plans.

If this is a plan that would suit you, be sure to shop around for the best rates and plans.

Bridge Financing

You have your current home listed for sale and started shopping for a new home. You have found the exact home you are looking for but you haven't yet sold your current home. What can you do?

You can make an offer making it subject to the sale of your current home. If that is accepted, the seller still has the option to market the home and accept another offer. If that seller has accepted another offer, he has to inform you and you have a stipulated amount of time to remove your condition and secure your new home.

I usually recommend to my buyers to arrange for bridge financing if they are going to make an offer subject to the sale of their current home. Bridge financing covers that gap between the sale of the current home and the purchase of a new home. The buyer is then in a position to remove the condition and acquire the new home before the sale of the current home.

Prior to making such a recommendation, I review market conditions with the buyer as well as the saleability of his home. If all is favourable, then bridge financing is a good option.

Use of RRSP towards Home Financing

This won't handle all your financing needs, but it can certainly contribute. The Government has made a provision for first time home buyer to withdraw up to $20,000 from their RRSP, tax free and apply it towards the purchase of a home. If a spouse also qualifies then the total can be $40,000.

This can be used for a down payment or towards the mortgage. Check with your professional for more details and the pay back plan.

Mortgage Approval in Writing

Once you have provided all the information, mortgage approval can usually be obtained in approximately 48 hours. This is the first condition that should be removed in a residential sale, since you don't want to spend any other money, such as a home inspection, until you know that you are eligible for a mortgage.

Some years ago, I had a client who was refused a mortgage after a so-called approval over the phone. My client ordered the home inspection and then found out the mortgage was not approved. Apparently, this mortgage person was busy and fell behind in processing the documents but assumed everything would go well and so indicated to my client that all was approved. We had no recourse because we had nothing in writing.

Consequently, I always request mortgage approval in writing from the financial institution. It is a protection for my client and it also indicates that I, as a REALTOR®, have done my due diligence.

Closing Costs

Aside from the down payment for your home purchase, you will also have to pay closing costs. Though the dollar amounts vary from area to area, the items may include:

Appraisal
Survey and/or Title Insurance
Home Inspection
Legal
Property Purchase Tax/Land Transfer Tax
GST/HST (new home)

Other Costs

There is certainly no shortage of costs! Here are a few more to keep in mind and to plan for.

Moving costs
Utility connection costs - phone-water-electric- cable etc
Cleaning costs
Renovation costs

Celebration costs!

Your Home Inspector

Robert Hughes

Your Home Inspector's Background

Engineer Technologist

In 1987 through Ryerson University – Toronto, I was certified as an Engineering Technologist.

Project Coordinator

I later became a Project Coordinator for a commercial construction company, specializing in large institutional construction.

Senior Forecast Analyst

I was a Senior Forecast Analyst in the program-planning department of a large corporation. This involved planning and monitoring projects including those related to the renovation and construction of company facilities.

Sales - Construction Materials

My involvement in the sale of commercial and residential construction materials on Vancouver Island, BC has been very helpful in my inspection work.

Home and Property Inspection

With my background in construction and engineering, I became interested in a career in Home and Property Inspection. I contacted the owner of Fleetwood Building Inspections (FBI). It was one of the largest professional inspection companies in the area doing business since 1992.

From the moment I went on my first home inspection, I was hooked! I worked as a contractor for the owner for 3 years.

Owner of Fleetwood Building Inspections (FBI)

I enjoyed the flexibility of schedule, different venues and the client and REALTOR® contacts. These things made every day new and interesting. I wanted to purchase the business and the owner was ready to sell and pursue other interests. The timing was right and I became the new owner of FBI.

Everyday Puzzle

For me, each house is a puzzle and a mystery just waiting to be solved.

I often have mixed feelings about an inspection. On one hand, I'm pleased to have found that 'hidden defect' that would have caused the buyer grief. And, on the other hand, I'm disappointed to have to bring bad news to someone who has their heart set on buying what they thought was a perfect house.

At this point, a proper perspective by the Inspector regarding the seriousness of the deficiency, or lack thereof, is very important in order for the buyer to make an informed decision. I strive to always present my findings in a balanced manner.

Current Status

As owner of Fleetwood Building Inspections (FBI), it is my goal to ensure that all home inspections are conducted thoroughly and with integrity.

I am licensed in the Province of British Columbia, a Registered Home Inspector, member of the Canadian Association of Home and Property Inspectors (CAHPI) for the last 5 years, and a past member of the National Certification Program for Home and Property Inspectors.

With on-going training, new innovations, products and discoveries in the construction industry, Home and Property Inspection continues to be an exciting and satisfying career.

Why Do I Need a Home Inspection?

Most people would never think about buying a used car without having a mechanic check it out first, but some buyers still buy a home for ¼ to ½ million dollars or more and have their Uncle Fred look at it for them. Not only does that put a lot of pressure and liability on Fred, but it also assumes he has read up on the latest in drainage, structural, electrical, plumbing, heating, roofing and ventilation problems.

That means you are spending all that money on a house based on Uncle Fred's knowledge and perspective.

More and more today, banks, mortgage lenders and insurance companies are demanding a home inspection before purchase. Most REALTORS® will strongly suggest a Professional Home Inspection to protect their clients.

By law, any paid Home Inspection in British Columbia, must now be done by a Home and Property Inspector licensed by Consumer Protection BC.

A Home Inspection Should NOT be Considered an Insurance Policy

It will not eliminate all risks associated with purchasing a home. It will however, provide you with a clearer understanding of a home's physical structure and systems and their visible deficiencies at the time of the inspection.

Major and Minor Issues

As a Home and Property Inspector, I concentrate on the identification of major problems (those costing $2000 and up) that may affect the house sale, such as structural movement, unsafe conditions, system failures etc.

I also check hundreds of minor items, which are noted as a courtesy during my search for the major issues. Not all minor deficiencies, especially cosmetic ones, will be noted, but you should end up with a list of important items that will need your attention.

What Does a Home Inspector Really Do?

When I get a call to do a Home Inspection for a buyer, I try to find out from the buyer and REALTOR®, as much as I can about the building and any concerns the buyer may have. I ask for a copy of the MLS® feature sheet and the Property Condition Disclosure Statement plus any other pertinent information available.

> "Every building is a new mystery that we have to solve in 3-4 hours"

Every building is a new mystery that we have to solve in 3-4 hours. Of course, the larger the building the longer it will take. All homes have deficiencies, both hidden and obvious. A Home Inspector is like a detective looking for clues to advance his understanding of the underlying problems that the house may contain.

With approximately 500 items to check in a few hours, we won't necessarily see every scratch and sticky door, but that unsafe electrical panel, for instance, if it's accessible, will get checked!

By choice, I use a checklist type of reporting system for most homes. It may not be as fancy as the computer driven report format that we use on larger inspections but it forces me to a strict regime of inspecting every accessible area and major component. It allows me to concentrate my time on inspecting rather than spending half my time (or more) on trying to produce and print a computer report. If there are important hidden deficiencies on roofs, in attics or crawl spaces, I have a slideshow available for the buyer, from the inspection pictures taken.

During an inspection, I check the site, the exterior, the roof, decks, stair supports, garage, foundation and structure, attic, plumbing, heating and electrical systems.

I try to operate as many things in the house as possible, including a sampling of doors, windows, lights, outlets and all baseboard heaters. We look at walls, floors and ceilings for clues to structural problems and leaks (not so easy when everything is covered up and often obscured by owners' personal effects).

Generalist vs. Specialist

> "...a 3 to 4 hour house inspection could never cover all that would be involved..."

A Home Inspector is a generalist. Many in the public, including the trades, often think Home Inspectors are a combination of a code inspector, electrician, plumber, roofer, drain specialist, heating and air-conditioning expert, structural engineer etc. No one fits that bill and a 3 to 4 hour house inspection could never cover all that would be involved in a specialized inspection in those disciplines.

What we will do, however, is note issues with these and other house components and where necessary, recommend further examination by a specialist in that area.

For example, if I see evidence of moisture in a basement, I may recommend that a drain company should check the perimeter drains for proper function. If the crawl space house framing is not done properly or is unsafe, I would recommend that a carpenter and/or a foundation specialist should correct the situation.

Maintain vs. Replace

> "…even a new roof can leak with the onset of extreme weather and damage."

I may report that with some repair and ongoing maintenance, a component such as an older roof can have its life expectancy extended. Keep in mind that even a new roof can leak with the onset of extreme weather and damage. We cannot warranty or guarantee a roof. Even professional roof inspection companies may hesitate to certify a roof installed by someone else, even after a two-hour concentrated inspection, especially a wood roof. There is too much that cannot be seen and even something as small as a pinhole can start a roof leaking.

Often roofing companies will suggest complete replacement rather than a repair for older roofs, to avoid callbacks and liability concerns even though several years may be left in the roof. Typical life spans though, can be given for a particular type of roof along with the current roof age if known.

The Canadian Association of Home and Property Inspectors (CAHPI) has 'Standards of Practice' that must be adhered to by its members, detailing all the areas inspectors can or cannot inspect. This standard is available on line at the CAHPI website. (www.cahpi.bc.ca)

What a Home Inspector Can't Do!

> "It's not our house or your house yet - we only have permission to look at it!"

An inspector is a guest in someone else's home. He is conducting a visual inspection. He cannot knock holes in walls or move equipment, furniture or carpets around. It's not our house or your house yet - we only have permission to look at it!

The Inspector looks for clues to past problems in the home but sometimes those clues are not evident until carpets are lifted, furniture removed or finishes altered.

Apart from the time it would take, I would not feel comfortable emptying an entire closet to check for mould or move a loaded bookcase to get access to an electrical panel.

Home and Property Inspectors are not allowed to light gas pilot lights in case there is an unreported leak or faulty equipment.

We cannot damage any property, which may be required for opening a sealed attic hatch or hot water tank compartment, without the owner's permission.

Other areas can be inaccessible or too dangerous to enter, such as high, steep and/or slippery roofs, low confined crawl spaces, congested attic spaces etc.

I try my best in these areas, but always inform the buyer of any restrictions I may have had. Please note when access is restricted, we give you our best estimate of conditions based on what we can see. Several hours by a contractor with specialized equipment may yield additional information.

Home and Property Inspectors do not inspect well systems for capacity, water quality etc. We do not inspect hot tubs, septic, irrigation, sprinkler or perimeter drainage systems or check for underground oil tanks. All these items take specialized equipment by a certified service contractor.

All these limitations are clearly written in the report's inspection agreement, not as contractual language to hide behind, but to give the buyer a clear and comprehensive understanding of the inspector's inspection restrictions. If required, an advanced copy of the agreement can be obtained from the inspector.

Why Didn't the Inspector See It?

> "I could likely find more problems if I spent a half-hour under the sink..."

The Inspector examines hundreds of items contained in a home. Often storage items, overgrown shrubbery, cosmetic cover-ups such as filled in cracks or painting over moisture stains etc., can hide deficiencies.

Also looking under all the insulation in an attic, for example, is not practical – only a sample area is viewed. I could likely find more problems if I spent a half-hour under the sink or an hour disassembling the furnace as a contractor would – but the inspection would be at a much higher cost.

Often in older houses we will also see things, which strictly speaking, are not to present-day code, but are functional and safe as they stand. We don't necessarily flag those items as perhaps a tradesman might, other than to note possible unprofessional work.

Some Problems Can Only be Discovered by Living in a House

For example, a vacant house may not show high moisture reading on the tub tiles or floor near the toilet because of lack of use. Some shower stalls leak only when a person stands in the shower, but not when the tap is just turned on. Some roofs and basements only leak when specific weather conditions exist such as excessive or driving rain.

In addition, it is sometimes hard for buyers to remember the circumstances in the house at the time of the inspection. The weather may have been severe, there could have been many storage items and household effects everywhere, the furnace might not have been turned on because the air conditioning was operating etc.

I had a case where a house had termites but everything had been cleverly hidden with storage in a closet and a bed pushed against a wood panel wall to hide the damage.

Buyers are advised to read their Inspection Report carefully, do a final walk through when the owner has moved out and to consult their REALTOR® and/or the Inspector, if necessary.

> "And by the way… x-ray vision is still just too expensive."

And by the way… x-ray vision is still just too expensive. Infrared cameras, contrary to popular belief, cannot see inside walls. They only read surface temperatures and work best when there are large temperature differences from the outside to the inside (they may also pick-up temperature differences caused by moisture or large nests of insects or rodents in enclosed cavities).

Infrared camera inspection, however, is a separate kind of inspection requiring several hours examining the walls. It requires specialized training plus data analysis to provide any kind of comprehensive survey of a building. It is usually called for when symptoms of a problem start to appear which require further investigation.

The Inspector and the REALTOR®

We all accept referrals from professional service providers.

Lawyers will recommend an accountant, a doctor will refer to a specific specialist, an engineering firm will often deal with a particular group of contractors, or a general contractor with certain sub-trades. Concerns have been raised over business relationships between REALTORS® and Home Inspectors, sighting a possible conflict of interest when a REALTOR® recommends one or several specific inspectors.

Like everyone else, REALTORS® have worked with others in their industry and presumably have found the best inspectors who fit their particular style. How should the REALTOR®/Inspector relationship be viewed? Is there opportunity for abuse? There is always the opportunity but in such an instance both the REALTOR® and the Home Inspector would have to act unprofessionally.

To minimize such an occurrence even further, REALTORS® are instructed to recommend a minimum of three professionals to their clients from whom they can choose. In this way, the buyer can still take advantage of the REALTOR'S® experience with the Home Inspectors.

Don't forget, a Home Inspector takes responsibility for what he inspects. He is accountable for his inspection. A good inspector should, however, put any deficiencies found, into proper perspective. There will always be minor issues but the inspector's role is to focus on those areas that may ultimately be costly for the buyer. For example, it may be discovered that the furnace needs replacing. The buyer may not wish to take on this expense but the REALTOR® may suggest a re-negotiation of price that could satisfy both parties.

Most REALTORS® are concerned primarily with the satisfaction of their buyers and want them to be happy with their purchase. Rather than a risk for possibly losing the sale, the inspection can become a protection for the buyer and REALTOR® from future financial repercussions and dissatisfaction that might haunt them for years. A relationship with a good inspection company then becomes an asset for the REALTOR® who can be confident that their buyer will be given all the information available from the inspection in its proper context.

The good Home Inspector always works for the client regardless of how well he may know the REALTOR®. My job is to point out the deficiencies as well as the strong points in a building and present the evidence - not to sell the building to the client. We don't pass or fail the house, but rather provide all the important details so the buyer can make an informed decision.

> "…a professional lawyer or accountant would never 'cook the books'…"

Just as a professional lawyer or accountant would never 'cook the books' no matter how much they wanted your repeat business, in the same way a good and professional Home Inspector will give you the straight goods, clearly describing what he has found and its implications.

A business relationship between a good REALTOR® and Home Inspector, in my opinion, is probably the best situation a buyer can have for consistency and thoroughness. The Inspector can trust the REALTOR® to act in the best interests of the buyer, and the REALTOR® knows he/she can trust the Inspector to provide a balanced report on what the building contains.

The Inspector and the Buyer

Sometimes a buyer wants to accompany the Inspector during the entire Home Inspection. Although some may encourage it, this can be distracting to the process of the Inspection.

The home is already built and enclosed and we are like detectives looking for clues to concealed problems. Having someone pointing out and asking questions about numerous things (many of which may be obvious) can make it difficult to puzzle out the subtle hints of a possible hidden problem.

> "I find it much better to walk the buyer through the house after I complete the Inspection…"

I find it much better to walk the buyer through the house <u>after</u> I complete the inspection, giving them my full attention and showing them the actual deficiencies I have found after considering <u>all</u> the evidence. It's often not until we add together all the clues that a true picture of the problem evolves.

With a walk through <u>during</u> the Inspection, the Inspector runs the risk of telling the buyer one thing at the start of the inspection and something different at the end, which adds to the sometimes overwhelming amount of information presented, thereby confusing the buyer.

The custom is for the Home Inspector to have access to the home through the buyer's REALTOR® or through the seller as he is on his way out. I am usually alone in the seller's home. The buyer's REALTOR® then returns at a designated time with the buyers for the walk through.

From time to time, I will have a buyer wanting to show up early before the inspection is completed. I try to discourage buyers from attending prior to the walk through, except with the REALTOR'S® permission.

Not only is it a distraction for me, but also I'm responsible for the security of the home and its contents during the inspection. It's not fair to the owner to have the buyer and entourage wandering through their home while I have my head up in the attic or I'm sleuthing out the crawl space.

The Inspector and the Owner

I'm often surprised how home sellers don't seem to understand the Home Inspection process. This is an opportunity for the buyer to discover if he has made a viable choice. Some owners seem to view the inspection as an invasion of their privacy and an unnecessary bother rather than their chance to make an impression and seal the deal.

"Some owners seem to view the inspection as an invasion of their privacy..."

Occasionally, an owner will insist on staying for the whole inspection, not trusting the Inspector to be in the house alone. Ironically the seller will allow his house to be open to all the REALTORS® in the city as well to strangers during an

Open House, but is very wary of the Inspector. Our requirements in British Columbia are similar to REALTORS®. We have to be licensed and insured and if we are dishonest we would be out of business in no time.

As an owner, try to tear yourself away from your house for 3 or 4 hours for the inspection. You'll survive the separation from your house and possessions and it will allow the inspector to move easily throughout the house without worrying about invading your personal space. I'm not going to rob you or snoop through your personal items.

> "I really don't care if you wear red long johns…"

After hundreds and hundreds of inspections, I really don't care if you wear red long johns, only whether your attic has mould or your hot water tank is leaking. With 500 or 600 items to check and the buyer and REALTOR® coming soon, it takes all of my attention to finish on time and have an accurate report ready.

For the inspection and walk through, the owner is typically encouraged by their own REALTOR® to allow the buyer the privacy of hearing about the inspection and seeing the house again, before they make a final decision.

Home Inspection Myths and Misconceptions

A Home Inspector, during his inspection will find everything wrong with my house and everything that could go wrong for at least a few years.

We don't have magic wands or crystal balls. We are testing systems for function and looking for visible deficiencies for the major house components. Things like foundation cracks, unsafe electrical panels and leaky roofs. We can't predict the future. A furnace could be operating well and then suddenly stop due to a worn out part. A roof which had never leaked before could have a hidden surface finally wear through after heavy rains.

I'm anxious to see if the septic and well are working properly and whether the perimeter drains are okay. I'll see what the inspector finds out during the inspection.

A Home and Property Inspector is not trained, nor does he carry the specialized equipment required for thoroughly checking wells, irrigation systems, septic systems perimeter drains or any underground plumbing. These are all unique and lengthy inspections by themselves.

Inspectors have moisture meters, so if there is moisture in the floors, walls or ceilings, he'll find it.

A moisture meter is only one tool we have. It is used in areas that we suspect could have problems, not the whole house. These devices are not fool proof. They only register moisture up to ¾" to 1" below the surface and the readings are affected by underlying concrete, metal etc.

The inspector checked our old roof, so we shouldn't have any leaks this year.

A Home Inspector looks for damage or holes in the roof where visible and any leaking that may be indicated inside the house. He is basically giving you the heads up on anything that looks unusual. He cannot give you a guarantee or warranty. A roofing inspection company can spend a lot more time and effort studying the roof surface and may provide a certification of its future performance. In most cases, to avoid liability, they will recommend roof replacement for older roofs.

One inspection company is the same as the next, so price is really what matters. I only want them to check for major concerns anyway.

Home Inspectors who are members of the Canadian Association of Home and Property Inspectors, are required to do a complete inspection according to the association's Standards of Practice. Checking the smaller components can often lead to finding a major problem. i.e. in an old house, checking the electrical outlets may lead us to suspect active knob and tube wiring. A badly operating plumbing fixture may indicate hidden unprofessional plumbing or investigating an under stair storage area could reveal a termite infestation etc.

The Walk Through

After I've finished my inspection and documented my findings, at the designated time, the buyer and their REALTOR® arrive for the walk through. We literally walk around the outside and inside of the house as I point out the various deficiencies as well as the beneficial highlights that I have found.

I find a physical walk through is much more informative and less confusing than trying to puzzle out pictures that may not properly illustrate the deficiency or its actual location. If there are inaccessible areas with problems such as attics or crawl spaces, for greater clarity I may decide to provide a slide show to illustrate these deficiencies.

The walk through is dedicated entirely to the buyer who is encouraged to ask questions.

The buyer is presented with his/her completed inspection report at the end of the inspection. The report contains not only deficiencies found but also an inventory of the building's attributes, diagrams and line drawings of some of the more common building problems, a Purchasers Pre-closing Inspection Checklist, a Home Maintenance Checklist, the Canadian Association of Home and Property Inspectors 'Standards of Practice' and our Standard Agreement and Invoice.

If questions arise after the inspection, the buyer is free to give me a call for further information.

As a Home Inspector, I do not provide any judgement with respect to property value and the home does not receive a pass or fail. The inspection facts are presented in context to the buyer to help him make a confident and informed decision with a clearer understanding of the condition of the home's structure and systems.

Your Lawyer - for Buyer

Kelly Orr

Your Lawyer's Experience

Law or Music or Both?

I have been practicing law for twenty-five years now. I knew from the time I was in high school that I wanted to go into law and made my plans accordingly. Although I was heavily involved in music during school and was counselled to pursue music at University, I wanted to take courses which would better prepare me for law school.

Having said that, while taking my undergraduate courses, I also sang in two or three choirs, played in two jazz bands and a pep band that supported the University of Victoria basketball teams.

I wrote my Law School Admission Test (LSAT) while in second year of my undergraduate program to give myself time to rewrite in case my scores were not up to my expectations. However, I achieved a fairly high score on my LSAT so decided to let it stand. I applied to law school while in my third year of undergrad, expecting to be denied entrance until I had completed my degree but wanting to have a file opened in my name at a number of schools.

Much to my surprise, I was accepted at five of the six schools I had applied to without having attained my undergraduate degree and, after some deliberation, for a number or reasons I decided to attend UVIC.

Law School

Once I had completed law school it was time to article.

I was fortunate enough to find an articling position in Victoria that turned out to be an amazing experience. I was given my own files from the outset and was expected to figure things out for myself, rather than simply doing menial tasks for other lawyers.

I articled for a lawyer who practiced real estate and commercial law, but also did work for other lawyers in the firms I was with. As a result, I had a well rounded experience which enabled me to decide which areas of the law appealed to me and which did not.

I was also lucky enough to work with many legal assistants who were very patient in helping me to understand the documentation process and would allow me to assist in that process (even though it would probably have been easier for them to do it themselves). This experience proved to be invaluable when I later went into business for myself, and in fact throughout my legal career, as I was able to understand and do the legal assistant's position as well.

Business Experience

Having attended University right out of high school, and then law school after only three years of undergrad, I graduated from law school while still quite young, and having little life experience and no business experience.

As a result, upon graduation I applied for a job as the Executive Director of the Victoria Home Builders Association. This allowed me to learn a lot about business, bookkeeping and other skills that I would need to run my own business. I also learned a lot about building, land development and real estate which I would need in my practice.

While I was with the Victoria Home Builders Association we won an award for the most improved chapter of the Canadian Home Builders Association and I received an award for the top Executive Director nationally.

My Own Law Office

After several years with the Victoria Home Builders Association, I decided it was time to put my degree to its proper use so I opened my own law office. I focused my practice primarily on real estate and land development, but also worked in other solicitor-related areas of the law such as corporate and commercial, contracts, wills, estates and trusts. I continued with my private practice for 15 years and built a thriving business.

Joining Browne Associates

After so many years in private practice with its challenges, it was time for a change.

When I met Dunstan Browne, through mutual friends, and he asked me to join his firm, I did. I have been with Browne Associates since.

Law with a Touch of Music and the Arts

Although I practice law full time, I also direct a choir. Over the years, I have participated in improv theatre as well as conventional theatre and musical theatre, both on stage and as music director.

My love of music and the arts has led me to expand my practice to include some entertainment law, mostly in the areas of music and film. This, in turn, has led to an opportunity to participate in the making of a movie here in Victoria, an incredibly fun and rewarding experience.

You Have Accepted Offer

So you have decided to purchase a new home. You have worked with a REALTOR® to prepare an offer and it has been accepted. Well, now what do you do?

One of the first things you will need to do is to make sure you know exactly what it is that you are buying, and to do this it is often wise to speak to a lawyer. You will need to have a lawyer in any event as your lawyer is the one who will ensure that your purchase is properly completed, that title to the property gets registered in your name, that you receive that title to the property, free and clear of any charges or encumbrances. Your lawyer will ensure that all details are in order so that, barring any intervening problems, you will be able to resell the property later on without any legal difficulties.

Selecting Lawyer

But how do you find a good lawyer. If you have not already been dealing with, or are not friends with a lawyer, the best way to find one is through a referral, either from your REALTOR®, your banker or a friend. By seeking a referral you will know you are dealing with someone in whom others have confidence, which should in turn give you confidence from the outset.

Establishing Contact

Your first contact with me may be at your instigation, when you call to ask me if I will review your title with you and discuss the charges that appear on the title. Reviewing the title is always a wise course of action. However, if the title to the property is very clean (not many non-financial charges that your REALTOR® is concerned about), you may simply let your REALTOR® send me the initial paperwork.

Once I receive the contract of purchase and sale, I will send you a letter, thanking you for choosing to deal with me and giving you a very basic outline of what to expect. If we get together to review your title, I will have printed out all of the charges that appear on title (unless you or your REALTOR® advises me that you have copies of the documents already) and we will sit down to discuss what they mean and how they will affect the marketability of your title.

Charges on Title - Removable

Some of the charges you may see on a title are:

1. Mortgages are probably the most common charges that appear on a title. A mortgage is a charge in favour of a lender to secure the repayment of a loan. If you are purchasing a property which has a mortgage on the title, the solicitor for the seller of the property will be put on an undertaking to pay out and obtain a discharge of the mortgage. Therefore, unless you

are going to assume a mortgage, it will not adversely affect your title as it will be removed upon the completion of your purchase.

2. Similarly, liens and judgments are financial charges which may appear on a title and which will be subject to an undertaking to remove upon completion of a sale.

Charges on Title - Not Removable

On the other hand, there are a number of charges which may appear on title and which "run with the land" or, in other words, which will remain on title even after a sale.

The following are some British Columbia examples:

Some of these charges include:

1. Undersurface Rights or Exceptions and Reservations are similar charges. When you purchase a property in British Columbia, you obtain title to the surface of the property (and to a certain extent, the air space above the surface) only. In most cases, the mineral rights beneath the surface of the property belong to or are controlled by the crown (or the provincial government). In some instances, however, the mineral rights may be controlled by the Esquimalt and Nanaimo Railway, the Director of Soldier Settlement or, in rare cases, by an individual.

    The mineral rights may then be obtained by any individual who holds a Free Miner's Certificate, which authorizes that individual to gain access to private property to explore for minerals. Although it is true that the owner of the surface rights and the owner of the undersurface rights have competing interests and claims, there are many regulations in place to safeguard those competing interests. For instance, the owner of the undersurface rights cannot bring equipment onto private property and disturb the land to explore for minerals without first submitting a plan and obtaining a permit from the government. Such a permit will not be issued with respect to private property without first notifying the surface owner and affording the surface owner an opportunity to express concerns. In addition, the surface owner has a right to compensation for the use of his land, as well as a right to assurance that the surface of the land will be put back in its original condition upon completion of the mining or exploration work and to this end the permit holder will be required to post a reclamation bond. As far as the amount of compensation is concerned, this may be determined by agreement between the parties or, where an agreement cannot be reached, by way of an arbitration process which will ensure the rights of all parties are protected.

In a well developed urban area, the chances that someone will exercise the undersurface rights are remote and, therefore, this type of charge really has little affect on your title to the land.

2. An easement is a charge against a piece of property whereby the owner of the property which is subject to the charge (the 'servient owner') grants permission to the owner of an adjacent property (the 'dominant owner') to have access to or use of a portion of the servient owner's property for some specific purpose. For example, the servient owner may grant the dominant owner permission to drive over a portion of the servient owner's driveway to gain access to the dominant owner's property.

    Another common use for an easement is where a portion of a building on the dominant owner's property encroaches onto the servient owner's property. An easement can be used to allow the encroachment to remain in place. Although, normally, if there is a fire or some other catastrophic event which destroys the building that encroaches, the easement will fall away and the dominant owner will be required to rebuild the structure in such a way as to avoid an encroachment.

An easement is simply a permission to use and does not transfer any portion of the title to the servient owner's property to the dominant owner. In addition, there are often rules or conditions which attach to an easement to ensure each party's rights are protected, in particular a rule which makes the dominant owner responsible to repair any damage done to the servient owner's property by the dominant owner in exercising his rights under the easement.

An easement, however, may restrict what you can do with your property. For example, normally you cannot build a permanent structure on an easement area. In addition, if an easement is to provide permanent access, you cannot usually park a vehicle on the area which is to provide that access.

An easement is a charge which is said to 'run with the land'. In other words, if the dominant owner sells his property the buyer will buy the dominant land with the easement attached and will become the new dominant owner. Although an easement is not usually seen as something which will adversely affect the marketability of your property, you will want to know the nature of an easement to ensure that your plans for the property are not affected.

3. A Statutory Right of Way or SRW is similar to an easement except that there does not need to be an adjacent property which benefits from the charge. In fact, an SRW is often in favour of a local government or a utility company and it gives the local government or utility company the right to enter upon property and disturb the property if need be in order to maintain or repair water lines, sewer lines, power lines, telephone lines and the like.

Again, there are normally rules which require any damage done to the property by representatives or employees of the local government or utility company, in exercising their rights under the SRW, to be repaired so that the property is put back into the same or similar condition to what is was prior to the exercise of the SRW.

An SRW is similar to an easement in that you normally can't build on or otherwise interfere with an SRW area. In addition, although an SRW shouldn't affect the marketability of your property, you will want to know where it is and what sorts of restrictions are placed on the area affected by the SRW.

4. A Covenant or a Restrictive Covenant, as it sounds, is a charge which restricts what you can do with your property. For example, it may restrict you from building within a certain distance from a body of water or some other element which could be hazardous to a dwelling or it may restrict the square footage or height of a building.

    Often a covenant is imposed by a local government, or it may be imposed by a developer in the form of a set of building restrictions which set out what types of building materials may be used, or what types of features cannot be installed, such as clotheslines or satellite dishes, or even how many vehicles may be parked in an open driveway.

    Again, this is a document that you want to be familiar with so you can be certain that if you have particular plans for your property, you will not be frustrated by existing restrictions.

These are merely examples of what may be on title. Other jurisdictions may have charges specific to their areas. These examples should assist you in ensuring that you ask the right questions of your own lawyer when making a real estate purchase.

Assessing and Understanding Your Other Conditions

Once you understand what all the charges on your property are and how they will affect your ownership, we will determine whether or not you should remove the subject to title condition from your offer.

You will also need to work to obtain your financing, your home inspection, confirmation that you are able to obtain insurance coverage, or whatever else is required to fulfill the other conditions precedent so that you can sign the addendum which removes your conditions and makes the Contract of Purchase and Sale final and binding.

Binding Contract of Purchase and Sale

Once you have a binding Contract of Purchase and Sale, I will receive the signed and accepted Contract, along with all addendums to that Contract, the property condition disclosure statement, and a summary sheet which outlines the nature of your transaction. You should also advise your banker or lender that I will be acting for you so that he or she can send me instructions to prepare your financing documents.

The Legal Process

After I receive real estate and mortgage instructions, I review the documents very carefully to make sure I am familiar with all the details of your transaction and then I can start to prepare for completion.

My first job will be to gather information required for documentation. For example, I will need to contact you to get your full names (including middle names) and occupations, your birth date and social insurance number (if you will be claiming a new home buyers exemption for the Property Transfer Tax, which I will discuss in more detail later), and where you will be obtaining your home insurance.

In addition, if there is more than one of you buying, I will need to know whether you wish to be registered on the title to the property as Joint Tenants or as Tenants in Common. If you are registered as Joint

Tenants, it means that you both own an equal share of the entire equitable interest in the property and if one of you should die, your interest in the property transfers to the other person by survivorship.

If you are registered as Tenants in Common, normally a division of interest is set out, for example, an undivided ½ interest each, or one person has an undivided 2/3 interest and the other an undivided 1/3 interest, or one person has an undivided 1/100 interest and the other has an undivided 99/100 interest. This latter division of interest is normally used where both people need to be registered on the title in order to qualify for a mortgage, however, one of you may qualify for a first-time home buyer's exemption from Property Transfer Tax (as discussed later) and so you want that person's percentage interest to be higher in order to maximize the benefit of the exemption.

I will then contact the municipality where your property is located to determine how much the property taxes for the year were (or will be) and if those taxes were paid. I will also determine if a home owner's grant was claimed.

A home owner's grant is available to persons who own a property as their principal residence. If you are under 65 and own your home, you will be entitled to receive a basic grant toward your property taxes. If you are over 65 you will be entitled to an additional grant. I will advise you of the specific dollar amount of any grant for which you may qualify.

Once we determine the property tax information, an adjustment for the amount of taxes that were paid will be made on the respective Statements of Adjustments (which I will discuss further later) so that each of the seller and the buyer will pay a proportionate amount of the property taxes based on the number of days in the year that they owned the property.

In addition, if it turns out that the property taxes should have been paid but were not, or that there are outstanding utilities owing with respect to the property, I will but the seller's lawyer on appropriate undertakings to pay.

If you are purchasing a condominium, townhouse or other strata property, I will also need to determine that all strata fees have been paid and the amount of the monthly strata levy (an adjustment of which will also be reflected on the Statements of Adjustments). Again, if there are any unpaid amounts which should have been paid, this will be handled by way of solicitors undertakings imposed on the seller's lawyer so that when you become the owner of the property, all amounts owing with respect to the property will be paid and current and all accounts will be in good standing.

Preparing Documents

Once I have collected all the preliminary information, my job will be to prepare the appropriate documents to send to the seller's lawyer. These documents will include:

1. The Form A Freehold Transfer which, upon completion, will be filed in the Victoria Land Title Office (in person or online) to transfer the title to the property from the Seller's name(s) to yours;

2. The appropriate Goods and Services Tax (GST) or where applicable the Harmonized Sales Tax (HST) declaration(s), which will set out why GST/HST is not applicable or, if you are purchasing a new house and GST/HST does apply, will set out how the GST/HST was calculated and will include an application for a new housing rebate if you are entitled to receive it;

3. A Canadian residency declaration in which the Seller warrants that he is a Canadian resident within the meaning of the Income Tax Act. If a seller is not a resident of Canada, I will place his solicitor on an undertaking to withhold 25% of the sale price pending receipt of a clearance certificate from the Canada Revenue Agency (CRA). This is for your protection if the Seller fails to remit the appropriate amount of income tax on any capital gains which are realized from the

sale of the property, you, as the buyer of the property, could become liable to pay any income tax owing;

4.   A statutory declaration respecting a survey certificate, which states that a survey certificate which has been provided by the Seller (and is, therefore, not new and current) still accurately reflects the state of the property and that there have been no renovations or additions or construction on the buildings on the property such that the building envelope would have changed.   Again, this is for your protection so that you can know that a survey certificate provided to you by the Seller is still accurate.   This can also save you some money in that if an existing survey is available with a statutory declaration, you will not have to order a new survey certificate.   These days, almost all mortgage lenders are requiring that a survey certificate or title insurance be provided as part of a mortgage package (I will provide more information on this later);

5.   If the property is a strata property (whether a condominium, a townhouse or a bare land strata) I will ask the Seller's lawyer to provide us with a Form F and Form B as provided for in the Strata Property Act.   These documents provide assurances that all strata fees for the property you are purchasing have been paid and that the Strata Council will not file a lien against your property.   The Form B also provides information and assurances that there is no litigation pending against the Strata Corporation, that there have been no special assessments levied against the property that you may be responsible to pay, that the Strata Corporation has collected and retains the appropriate contingency fund, and other such items;

6.   A Vendor's Statement of Adjustments which sets out what you have agreed to pay for the property, what has already been paid by way of a deposit, what adjustments need to be made for Property taxes, utilities, rentals, strata fees or other adjustable items;

These documents will be sent to the seller's lawyer with a letter which confirms a number of details of the transaction and which imposes a number of undertakings on the seller's lawyer. These undertakings will include a requirement to pay out of the sale proceeds sufficient funds to require any party who has filed a mortgage or other financial encumbrance against the title to the property to release or discharge their financial encumbrance.

Other undertakings may be to pay out of the sale proceeds any annual charges that the seller should have paid but are still outstanding, or to hold back funds from the sale proceeds pending receipt of a clearance certificate in the event the seller is not a resident of Canada, or pending the expiry of a builders' lien holdback period in the event the seller had work done on the property within 45 days of the completion date.

Lawyers undertakings seem like a simple promise to act but, in fact, are much more onerous than a simple promise, as a lawyer who breaches an undertaking is subject to severe sanctions from the law society, if not actual disbarment. Accordingly, the process of real estate conveyancing involves many undertakings which are imposed by and on each lawyer in the transaction to properly protect our clients.

Documents for Your Signature

After documents have gone to the seller's lawyer, I will prepare a number of documents for you to sign, including:

Property Purchase Tax- Land Transfer Tax

Property Transfer Tax also known as Land Transfer Tax in some jurisdictions, as it sounds, is a tax which is paid at the time an application is made to transfer a property or an interest in a property from one person to another.

The tax is payable on the fair market value of the property so if you have agreed to purchase a property for something less than fair market value due to a close relationship between you and the seller, or due to your providing the seller with some consideration for the property other than cash, you will still have to calculate the tax payable on the fair market value of the property. Fair market value is an amount that a person would be willing to pay in the open market for a property.

Normally if you have made an offer to purchase a property which was listed for sale through a real estate agent, the amount you have offered to pay will be deemed to be fair market value as long as the sale completes within a reasonable time after the offer was made. In circumstances where a long period of time has passed or where you are not dealing in an open market situation, normally the current assessed value of the property as determined by the BC Assessment Authority may be used as the fair market value.

For example in BC, presently the Property Transfer Tax is 1% of the first $200,000 of value of the property plus 2% of the balance of the value of the property over $200,000. So, for instance, if you are purchasing a property for $450,000.00 you would pay 1% of the first $200,000, or $2,000 plus 2% of $250,000, or $5,000 for a total tax of $7,000. This tax varies from jurisdiction to jurisdiction but be aware that you will be subjected to such a tax -- there are some exemptions.

Exemptions to this tax generally relate to previous home ownership. Your lawyer will advise you if any exemptions are available to you. Generally, there is a first time home buyer exemption which is available only if you have never before owned an interest in a principal residence anywhere in the world. There are a number of qualifying factors which can include a purchase price threshold, a size threshold and the fact that it should be used as your principal residence. Again, your lawyer can give you the specifics in your jurisdiction.

In addition, there are a number of personal qualifications such as Canadian citizenship (or permanent residency), residency requirements in your province which may be up to 12 months prior to your purchase or it may relate to filing provincial income tax and never having received a first-time home buyers exemption before.

I will calculate the Property Transfer Tax on your behalf and, in consultation with you, will determine if you qualify for any exemptions. I will prepare the appropriate return and the amount of Property Transfer Tax you are required to pay will be reflected on your Purchasers' Statement of Adjustments.

Mortgage

Many people think that after they have gone to see their mortgage lender and signed documents at their office, the mortgage itself is either done or simply gets sent to the lawyer in a completed form.

In fact, once you have signed the documents at the lender's office, the lender then converts those documents to a set of instructions which are sent to my office. I must then prepare the actual mortgage documents, based on the instructions received from your lender and based on the lender's preferred format for preparation of documents, but always in a form which will be acceptable to the Land Title Office where the document will be filed.

In British Columbia, the primary mortgage document which will be filed is called a Form B and will set out who the borrower is (normally the same persons who will be registered as owners of the property), who the lender is, how much money you are borrowing, and the repayment details such as interest rate, amount and frequency of payments and that sort of thing. In many cases these days, due to privacy and other issues, many of the loan and repayment details will be reflected in documents which you sign either at the lender's office or at my office, but will not appear on the mortgage document to be registered as once registered, the mortgage becomes a public document.

Aside from the Form B, I will also prepare an acknowledgement of receipt of mortgage terms. The mortgage terms is a document that sets out the generic terms and conditions of a mortgage, such as what types of promises you are making to the lender and what the lender can do in the event that you break any of your promises or default under the loan. You will sign this document after I have given you a set of the mortgage terms, an order to pay which sets out how much money the lender has agreed to lend to you and any amounts which will be deducted from the mortgage advance for things such as a mortgage insurance premium, a lender's fee, and appraisal fee and that sort of thing.

Other Documents

Often there are many other documents, such as statutory declarations, disclosure statements, identification forms and that sort of thing, which must be prepared or reviewed to fulfill the lender's requirements.

Survey Certificate

Most lenders will also require that we obtain either a survey certificate or title insurance for the property being purchased (some lenders, but not many, require both). A survey certificate is a document prepared by a land surveyor which draws to scale an outline of the boundaries of your property and an outline of the shape of any buildings on the property and where the edges of those buildings are in relation to the edges of the property.

The real importance of a survey certificate is to show whether the building you are proposing to purchase actually sits wholly within the boundaries of the lot on which it is situated, or whether it extends over or encroaches onto a neighbour's property.

If there is an encroachment which has not been dealt with by way of an easement or other arrangement with the neighbour, you could be facing an expensive problem if you purchase the property and we would want to discuss your options at that point. The problem may not come to light until you go to sell the property and a prospective buyer obtains a survey certificate which shows the defect. This may lead to you having to do extensive renovations to remove the encroachment, or to you having to negotiate with the neighbour to purchase a portion of his property or obtain an easement.

A survey, therefore, is an important document, however, the cost for a survey certificate is quite significant and, accordingly, many people opt to get title insurance instead.

Title Insurance

Title insurance, as it sounds, is insurance against many defects in the title to your property. Often title insurance can eliminate the need for a survey certificate as long as you are not aware of any defects in the property which would have been revealed had you obtained a survey (an encroachment for instance). Title insurance policy will cover you for those defects if they come to light after your purchase is complete.

Title insurance can also protect you against errors in surveys or in many other documents which affect your title, or against zoning or permit infractions. Another area where title insurance can protect you is against fraudulent practices which jeopardize your title or encumber your title. If your mortgage company requires that you obtain title insurance you will have the option of only providing the insurance for the lender, or for a reasonable additional fee, you may choose to protect both the lender and yourself.

Mortgage Disclosure Statement

Of course, there are several documents which are ancillary to a mortgage, some of which may be provided by the lender and some of which I will prepare as well. These documents may include a mortgage disclosure statement which outlines many of the terms and conditions of the loan such as the interest rate, the amount and frequency of each payment, when the payments will be made, if there are any penalties for early repayment, any prepayment privileges you might have and, most importantly, how much it is going to cost you to borrow the money (or, in very simple terms, how much interest you will end up paying over the full term of the mortgage).

Statutory Declarations

Many lenders require statutory declarations which confirm that you will be using the property as a principal residence and that there is no secondary financing. All lenders have their own individual requirements, some of which are few and simple and others have very detailed and onerous requirements.

Goods and Services Tax/Harmonized Sales Tax Declarations

All Canadian provinces have either GST or HST. Upcoming shortly the GST will be converted to HST in some provinces currently paying GST. HST will have greater implications for new home buyers. The GST will be replaced with the HST and, as a consequence, the cost of new housing will increase. Rebates will be offered but they will generally not be sufficient to offset a tax increase. Consult with your lawyer for greater details when this tax is implemented.

If applicable -- GST/HST declarations set out whether GST/HST is payable and, if so, who will be responsible for paying it. GST/HST is applicable to a purchase of a new home only and normally you pay the GST/HST to the seller upon completion and the seller will be responsible for remitting the tax to Canada Revenue Agency.

If, however, you are a GST/HST registrant, you may opt to remit the tax directly as you may be able to claim input tax credits which will offset the amount you must pay. When you are buying a new home it is important to make it clear whether the price you are offering to pay includes the full GST/HST, or whether the price includes the net GST/HST (total GST/HST payable less the new housing rebate which the seller will credit to you on your Statement of Adjustments and then you will assign back to the seller) or whether the price is exclusive of GST/HST meaning that the GST/HST will be added to the price.

It is important to note that you must qualify for the GST/HST new housing rebate. To qualify you must be purchasing a new or substantially renovated home for use as your principal residence and you must be the first occupants of the property. The full amount of the rebate is only available for properties with a fair market value of $350,000.00 or less, however, a partial rebate is still available for properties with a fair market value in excess of $350,000.00 but less than $450,000.00. These figures may vary by jurisdiction.

Purchaser's Statement of Adjustments

This document sets out the monetary details applicable to your purchase. When you buy a property there are a number of items which must be adjusted. For example, I will make the appropriate inquiries to determine the amount of the property taxes which are levied against the property and whether or not those taxes have been paid for the year.

Property taxes can be a confusing element of a purchase because, although the property tax year is a calendar year, or January 1st to December 31st, property taxes are due and owing on the first business day in July. Therefore, if you are scheduled to complete your purchase sometime between January 1st and the first business day in July, you will be responsible to pay the property taxes for the year.

However, if you do not complete your purchase until, say, April 14th, the seller should have to pay the taxes for the portion of the year that he owned the property, or for the 104 days between January 1st and April 14th. On the other hand, if your purchase is scheduled to complete sometime between the first business day in July and the 31st of December, the seller should have already paid the taxes, but will be entitled to receive a portion of those tax back from you pro rated as to the number of days in the year that you will own the property.

Making this adjustment also gives me the opportunity to ensure that if the seller should have paid the taxes, he did in fact do so and, if he didn't, I can ensure that he will pay them by putting his lawyer on appropriate undertakings to do so.

When checking on property taxes, I will also check to see that there are no outstanding utility accounts levied against the property. Some other items which may be adjusted on a Statement of Adjustments are strata fees, rental income and damage deposits, or any other prepaid items which relate to the property.

So the overall document will set out the items you have to pay, such as the purchase price, your share of annual fees that the seller has already paid, survey or title insurance costs, miscellaneous costs such as the cost of obtaining an insurance binder, and legal fees and disbursements. Then the document will set out the amounts you have already paid, such as the deposit or amounts that will be coming from someone else, such as mortgage proceeds from the lender or the seller's share of annual fees that you will be responsible for paying. At the end the document will set out how much additional money I will need from you in order to complete the transaction. This is essentially the balance of your down payment, plus or minus the adjustments I have talked about.

Your Appointment with Me

Once your documents have all been completed, I will call to make an appointment for you to attend and sign the documents. We will discuss how much time you should set aside for this appointment, as I prefer not to have to rush through the process.

Length of Time

If you have purchased property in the past, normally the signing process is quicker as you will likely not have as many questions or need things explained in as much detail as a first-time home buyer. The other factor that will determine the length of the process is the number and length of documents your lender requires to be completed and signed as well as the number of questions you will ask during our discussions. I encourage my clients to ask questions as they occur to them because if you wait until the end of our discussion you may have forgotten what it was you wanted to ask.

If you are a first-time home buyer, you should plan to spend a minimum of one hour or preferable one and a half hours in order that we can go through all the documentation in detail and can be sure that you will leave my office understanding all of your rights and responsibilities.

Often, however, there is a lot of information to take in and some people need time to properly assimilate the information. You will be given copies of most of the documents that you sign and I always tell my clients that they should feel free to call me with any questions they may come up with once they have had time to reflect upon all the information we have discussed, even if it is after the actual completion date.

I have had a number of occasions when clients have come to my office, for instance because they have gone to borrow more money from their bank, and when I explain to them that they will be signing a second mortgage document, they argue that they do not have a first mortgage yet. I then have to show them the title to the property and point out where the first mortgage is registered against it. Now these people were not stupid (in fact one set of clients were actually brain surgeons), however, when they signed documents with their other lawyers, it was not made clear to them exactly what they were signing (or they simply didn't understand but were afraid or embarrassed to ask).

I'm sure you have all been told or heard someone say that there are no stupid questions, and when it comes to buying and financing a home, that is especially true. A home will likely be the largest purchase of your life and a mortgage likely the largest debt you will incur. So it is really important that you understand exactly what your rights and responsibilities are, and what the consequences will be if you should fail to live up to those responsibilities.

Documents and Encumbrances

During our appointment we will discuss the details in all documents you have to sign, but we will also discuss the title transfer process in detail. If we haven't done so already, we will discuss the encumbrances that appear on your title, which ones will be removed by the seller's lawyer and which ones will remain on title. We will then talk about the nature of the charges which will remain on title and whether these are items which should concern you or not. I will ask you to confirm certain items for me to ensure I can protect you properly.

Seller's Residency

For example, I will ask you to confirm if you know whether the seller is a Canadian resident or not (as mentioned above, I also send a statutory declaration for the seller to swear which confirms his residency). This is important because non-resident sellers will be subject to capital gains tax and so the seller's lawyer must hold back sufficient funds to protect Canada Revenue Agency for this tax. If the seller does not pay the appropriate amount to Canada Revenue Agency a buyer can be held responsible for the amount and, therefore, it is vital that we know whether we should impose an undertaking on the seller's lawyer.

Seller's Representations/Promises

I will also ask you whether the seller made any promises or representations that do not appear on the Contract of Purchase and Sale. This is so we can determine whether these promises or representations can be enforced. For example, the seller may have promised to make certain repairs to the property or to remove certain garbage or other unwanted items from the property. If these promises have not been fulfilled prior to the completion date, we may be able to ensure their fulfillment by imposing an undertaking for a deficiency holdback which cannot be paid to the seller until he has fulfilled his commitment.

Recent Property Improvements

I will ask you if you are aware of any work which has been done to the property in the last 45 days which would entitle a contractor or supplier to file a builder's lien against the property. If such work has been done, again I will impose an undertaking on the seller's solicitor to maintain a holdback until the builders' lien holdback period has expired and then only to pay the holdback amount to the seller after having completed one further search of the title to the property which confirms that no liens or judgments have been filed against it.

Moving Advisories

I will also remind you, if you haven't already so done, to phone BC Hydro, Telus, Shaw cable or whoever you deal with to set up your utility accounts. You will need to contact your insurance agent to arrange for property insurance, and to make the appropriate arrangements to obtain keys from your real estate agent after we complete the transfer.

Conflict of Interest

At this point, I will also discuss with you the conflict of interest elements of the transaction. For example, many people think they can save money if the seller and buyer use the same lawyer. However, in most cases a lawyer cannot act for both the seller and buyer in the same transaction. The reason for this is that it is important that a lawyer's loyalties not be divided and that a lawyer is free to defend her client's best interests. If a lawyer has two clients with differing interests, it is difficult if not impossible to properly protect them both.

For example, if I am acting for a seller and on the scheduled completion date, the buyer cannot complete, I can protect my client by sending the appropriate letters stating that we are ready, willing and able to complete and imposing certain conditions for allowing the buyer to complete late, such as charging interest to the buyer to cover any additional interest or penalties the seller will incur due to the late completion.

On the other hand, if I am acting for the buyer and the seller is unable to complete as scheduled, I can advise the buyer of his options to negotiate terms and conditions for late closing, or to force the seller to complete if he is trying to renege on the deal or to sue for damages for failure to complete.

However, if I am acting for both the buyer and the seller in this situation, I cannot fully and effectively defend the buyer's best interests when I am also concerned about protecting the seller.

Representation re Buyer and Lender

In the case of a mortgage which is part of a simple transaction, however, a lawyer is allowed to, and usually does, act for both the lender and the borrower. This is because the interests of the lender and the borrower, at least in the beginning, are very similar. The borrower has already met with the lender and the two have agreed on the type of mortgage the borrower will get, along with the terms and conditions that apply to it. For example, will the borrower get a mortgage with a fixed rate of interest (say, 4.25% per annum) or a variable rate (such as prime + 1%). Will the borrower make a fixed payment which is blended principal and interest, or will the payment go up and down as the variable interest rate goes up and down, or will the borrower pay interest only. How long is the mortgage term and amortization period?

Once you have determined all these details with the lender, you will sign a loan agreement at the bank and then instructions will be sent to my office on the basis of that loan agreement. So it will be in the best interests of both you and the lender that the mortgage documents be prepared to reflect the agreement you reached. In addition, it will also be in both of your best interests that you receive good title to the property, free and clear of other encumbrances, that appropriate insurance is placed on the property, and that property taxes are paid and in good standing.

As you can see, the potential for divided loyalty is much lower here. However, I will also explain to you that, because I am acting for more than one party, it is not possible for me to keep your information confidential.

In other words, if you arrive at my office and advise me that you quit your job the day before, I would be bound to disclose that fact to the bank. I will also explain that if ever a conflict of interest does arise between you and the lender, for instance if you defaulted under the mortgage, whereas I would be able to attempt to help you resolve the matter with the lender, if you could not reach an agreement, I would not be able to continue to act for either you or the bank. I would be bound to send you both out to obtain new legal counsel.

Strata Corporations

If you are buying a strata property, I will confirm that you received all the pertinent documents, such as strata council and strata corporation meeting minutes, financial statements and budgets and information regarding common property, parking and storage locker assignments. We will discuss how a strata corporation works (particularly if this is your first experience living in a strata property) and what your rights and responsibilities are in relation to the strata corporation. I will have prepared a short document which outlines details about living in a strata property and this document will be included in your package of materials which I will give to you.

Financial Completion

At the end of the appointment (if we didn't already discuss this on the phone when we made our appointment) we will discuss your options for paying the balance we require to complete. Because these funds go into a trust account, we cannot simply accept a personal cheque so you will be required to bring in a certified cheque or a bank draft, or if you bank at an institution where our firm maintains a trust account, you may simply be able to instruct your bank to transfer funds from your account to our trust account.

Insurance Binder

Aside from preparing documents and meeting with you, there are a number of other details I will need to see to. For instance, I will write to your insurance agent to request a binder be sent to my office. An insurance binder is a document which confirms that you have purchased home insurance, and that in the event of an insurance claim, the insurer will pay the claim amount firstly to the mortgage lender and secondly to you. All lenders require that an insurance binder be obtained. I will also write to the surveyor to request a property survey be completed and/or I will order a title insurance policy.

Filing Documents and Completion

On the date set for completion of the transaction, I will take whatever steps are necessary to arrange for the registration of documents, either by way of an agent filing the documents at the Land Title Office, or by filing the documents myself online.

Once the documents are filed, I obtain what is known as a pending registration number and on that basis I will pay the balance of purchase proceeds to the seller's lawyer. I will also pay for certain items I obtained on your behalf such as an insurance binder and/or a survey certificate and/or title insurance. I will send a fax to the real estate companies involved in the transaction to provide registration numbers as evidence that we have completed the transfer of title so that the appropriate real estate agent will release keys to you and you can take possession. I will also prepare reports and document packages for both you and the lender.

After Completion

Following completion, your file remains open as I await receipt of confirmation from the seller's lawyer that any financial encumbrances which were on the property and which she was subject to an undertaking to remove, have in fact been removed. On receipt of that confirmation I will order a State of Title Certificate, copies of which will be sent to both you and the lender as evidence that you have good and valid title to the property, and then I will close my file.

Questions Arising after the Meeting

It takes time to digest this legal process so I am always open to follow-up questions.

There is never any additional charge for a telephone call to ask, "Kelly, what does this clause in the mortgage mean" or "can you explain once again what this item on the Statement of Adjustments is about". I am very committed to making sure you understand the legal process of buying real estate.

Your REALTOR® - for Seller

Vi Brown

Some sellers choose to sell their home on their own as opposed to enlisting an experienced real estate agent. I would like to shed some light on such an undertaking without the benefits of a professional.

For Sale by Owner (FSBO)

The main reason home owners attempt to sell their own property is to save the real estate fee. Many have sold their own property -- some successfully and some regretfully.

The less experienced the seller is with such a process, the greater the risks. I say this not to discourage anyone but simply to make you aware of some of the pitfalls.

Let me illustrate with an example.

Implications of Clauses

I was called by a seller to see if I could assist him in getting out of a contract. He was selling his home himself and had an offer in hand. The buyer drew up the contract and the seller didn't consult with anyone before signing.

The financing condition was 3 months long. He accepted the offer but did not fully comprehend the implication of the financing condition. In essence, it meant that the seller could not sell to anyone else for that 3 month period. And, if at the end of that period, the buyer could not get financing, the seller wasted 3 months. I suggested that the seller consult a lawyer.

Price

In the same example, I asked the seller his asking price and how he arrived at it. Apparently, he 'figured it out' and lowered it a bit because there were no real estate fees thinking that would make the property even more attractive.

I then asked him what the buyer offered. The seller said he didn't get as much as he hoped because the buyer reduced the price by an amount that represented real estate fees!

In a For Sale by Owner situation, buyers often present this argument. In fact, I have seen buyers who like to seek out FSBO properties to get a 'good deal'.

In many situations, the seller tries to save the real estate fee and the buyer feels he can get a better deal because he can offer a lower price because there is no real estate fee. Both parties are trying to save the real estate fee. Often the seller gets short changed.

Advertising

When you are selling your home, exposure is a must. You will have to do your own advertising in terms of lawn sign, newspapers and internet. It helps if you have some experience in writing ads and have some marketing skills. You will also need some photos. These all have costs attached.

Availability

You will then have to be available to take the calls and make appointments. You may also be exposed to people knocking on your door without having made an appointment.

If you are not comfortable pre-screening calls, you may be spending time with people who are not qualified to purchase.

Risks

Without pre-screening of any kind, there can be risks in inviting strangers to view your home.

My Own FSBO Experience

I indicated in the earlier part of this book that I sold my Fishing and Hunting Lodge without the benefit of a REALTOR®. This was only because I couldn't find an experienced REALTOR® in the recreational field in my area. Granted a lodge takes longer to sell than a home, but it took me about a year.

I also experienced the expense of advertising, trying to take the right kind of photos, wording the ads enticingly, fielding calls and making appointments.

One of the frustrating experiences involved pre-screening. I wanted to be sure that potential buyers were qualified to make such a purchase so I carefully asked them some questions pertaining to finances but did not receive clear answers. Potential buyers seemed to feel that their finances were not my business. I knew that obtaining financing for such a business was difficult and I tried to impress this point prior to them making the 4-5 hour trip north.

At the other end, I tried to diligently follow-up after each showing but again was not too successful. I generally received a variety of answers that didn't commit to anything.

Some of the showings I had seemed strange at first. I gradually found out that many that came up to see the lodge were frustrated with city life and their own circumstances. They had a moment where they thought 'escaping' to the north country was the answer. When they arrived and saw the realities, they soon got over their moment and realized that buying a fishing and hunting lodge was not the answer. I finally understood some of their remarks: -

"Gee that was a long way to come!" (I warned you)
"When are they paving this road?" (The 18 km road to the Lodge)
"You don't have any street lights!" (Just star light and moon light)
"Where are the moose?" (In the bush with the bears)
"Do you have the weekends off?" (Hardly!)
"Can we take a boat to see the lake?" (Write me an offer!)

This one made a real impression because they had a plan.

The family came with their 2 young children. I showed them around and explained various features of the property to the parents while their children played on the beach. They didn't ask many questions but at the end of my tour they asked if they could stay the weekend at no charge to 'experience the property'! The timing was great because when the children saw their parents returning from our tour, they came running and asked "Are we allowed to stay? -- are we staying?"

My response -- "Write me an offer!" They left.

The Last Word

If you choose to sell yourself, ask yourself some questions.

Do I know the market?
Is it a buyer's market or a seller's market?
Do I know where to best advertise?
Can I right a good ad?
What price should I ask?
Can I take appointment calls at my work?
Will it be enough to show only in the evenings and weekends when I'm home?
What if a buyer shows up at the door and my children are home alone after school?
Am I familiar with the paperwork?
Can I negotiate for myself?

Your home is one of your largest investments. Will you recognize potential problems during the process?

If you have any concerns, use the services of an experienced and professionally trained real estate agent. As a seller, you do not pay anything until your property is sold. Your REALTOR® absorbs all the expenses related to marketing your property - listing costs - internet advertising costs - print costs - sign costs - gas mileage - and much more. If your property doesn't sell, these costs are your

REALTOR'S® losses.

Often the benefits outweigh the costs particularly when you factor in a REALTOR'S® negotiating skills. Your REALTOR® certainly has the incentive to sell your property, combined with his/her training and experience, it is good value.

Contacting Your REALTOR®

You have decided to sell your home and you get in touch with me.
We have either worked together before or I have been recommended. It could also be that you have chosen to interview several REALTORS® so that you could find the right fit.

During our conversation, I determine whether you wish me to come prepared to list your property or you simply wish to first discuss market conditions and marketing strategies. You indicate that you want information and also to place your home on the market.

To that end, I ask some pertinent information about the property such as address, square footage, number of baths and bedrooms, heating, recent renovations, age of home, size of lot, how long you have lived there and the like.

I also ask you to have on hand all pertinent information such as taxes, assessments, survey certificates, permits and so on. We set up a time and date for the appointment and I ask all who are on title to be present.

Following are a couple of examples of appointments I had with sellers that were strangers and were located in rural areas.

Farm Experience

Some time ago when I was on floor duty, I spoke to a gentleman who wanted to place his farm on the market. He wanted someone to first come out and take a look. He wasn't too excited when I told him that I would be happy to come and see his farm. I asked for some additional information and he reluctantly gave it to me. I wasn't sure why he seemed reluctant but we set up an appointment anyway for the next day.

I did my homework, got some comparables that we could work with and I kept my appointment. It helped that I was somewhat familiar with the farm. It was a cloudy day and as I drove out to the farm, it began to rain.

The owner was standing by the barn as I drove in and pointed to where I should park. As I got out of my car, he looked me over and said "I can work with you! I thought you might be one of those prissy females trying to tip toe around the barn in your high heels watching where you step instead of paying attention to my farm!"

I had on rubber boots and rain gear. I was dressed for the occasion. The seller was delighted that I could go anywhere he could. A few days later he listed the property with me.

My Canine Assistant

When a potential seller calls, I try to gather as much information as possible before making an appointment to view and/or list the property. I also advise someone in my office or at home where I am going and how long I might be and promise to call when I am finished.

This one instance, a gentleman and his brother wanted to sell their seasonal cottage which was located in the middle of nowhere. I knew the area and was aware that it was very isolated. I told my husband where I was going and would have liked him to come with me but that was not possible so I took my German Shepherd, Kiska.

I should mention that Kiska was trained as a protection dog as we too lived in an isolated area. When I arrived at my destination, I left one of the windows in the vehicle wide open, in case I needed Kiska, and instructed her to stay.

The brothers were seated at a table on the porch so I suggested that we could chat there.

Kiska was seated in the front seat of my car watching. After some time, the brothers were amazed that my dog simply stayed in the vehicle without bounding out the window. They asked to see her so I just called her name and she jumped out the window and came up on the porch to meet and greet. We all went in to take a look at the inside of the cottage which I just listed.

I was pleased that all went well and I didn't need to engage the protection services of my canine assistant!

CMA - Comparative Market Analysis

After speaking to you over the phone, I use the information I gathered from you and search the data base to see if there was a previous listing. It is not likely since, in this instance, you have lived in the home for almost 20 years. I also obtain the property assessment. Since I am definitely listing the property, I also order a title search which is then billed to my account.

Before I start my CMA, I like to drive by the house and see exactly where it is located, take a photo and see the surrounding area.

I now have enough information to do my CMA. I will explain the contents of the CMA in the section entitled 'Meeting with the Seller'.

Preparing for the Listing Appointment

Since this is a listing appointment, I complete the Listing Contract as far as I can from the information I have already collected. Items, such as price, I leave till the appointment.

I gather all other paperwork that I will require. I have a 'Seller's Package' which contains useful information which I leave with the sellers.

I bring my real estate sign for the front lawn. Most municipalities no longer permit directional signs on street corners. If I do place a few directional signs, the municipality removes them and destroys them or charges me.

Since I have no sense of east, west, north or south, I always bring along a compass so that I know which direction the front and back of the house face -- an item on the listing contract.

I also bring along my camera. Often I take my own photos because I like to change around the photos in the print ads to match the text. For example, if one ad focuses on the acreage, I want a photo of the acreage - Is it cleared? Is it treed? I also like photos of the house from various angles to showcase different aspects and to eliminate the 'sameness' of an ad. Then, of course, I like a variety of photos for the internet.

I usually bring along my electronic measuring gadget, a 50 foot tape measure and decide later whether I will measure the home myself or hire someone to come and measure and draw up a floor plan.

The Appointment

I usually proceed in a specific sequence to make sure I cover everything. Once we have exchanged pleasantries, I ask for a tour of the house and property.

Home Tour

I ask the seller to give me a tour of the home and ask him to point out any significant elements that might be of interest to a buyer. I also ask that he point out any renovations that may have been recently done.

We then go outside and I ask about the location of property lines, sheds, fencing and so on.

I generally have a clip board on which I take my notes.

More Questions

I ask about any previous real estate experience they have had. This helps me to know what their expectations might be and how I can best meet them.

Have they had feedback after showings?

Besides providing timely feedback on showings, how much contact do they wish from me - weekly - more often - less often?

I also ask the sellers what initially attracted them to their home. This may be a marketing factor to draw others.

At this point, I discuss the market situation. I advise them whether it is a buyer's market (many properties from which buyers can select) or a seller's market (not enough properties for the demand). I touch on how sales have been going in their general area and anything else that may be pertinent at the time.

Home Staging

Having had a tour of the home, I noticed that there were some 'well lived in' areas. Other areas had a fair amount of clutter. Quite normal for a family that has been in the same home for 20 years!

I want to obtain the best price for them but I also realize that some buyers can't see beyond 'clutter' and 'lived in'. I discuss this with the sellers and suggest that they consult a home stager. A home stager can showcase this home to look its best. This can often produce a quicker sale and a better price.

The chapter entitled 'Your Home Stager' - written by Josée Lalonde will provide you with more information.

I then proceed to the more specific, the CMA.

The Property CMA - Comparative Market Analysis (Step 1)

The intent of a CMA is to assist you in selecting the optimum listing price range for your home.

To prepare a CMA, I use the MLS® System and select properties that are currently on the market which are similar to yours in terms of location, size, age and other relevant criteria. These are properties that will be competing with yours. It is likely that potential buyers, when house shopping, will be viewing those properties in conjunction with yours.

I utilize the same criteria to select homes which have recently sold. Recently sold is relevant to how quickly the market is changing. In a very fast moving market 'recent' may be a few days to a couple of weeks. Otherwise, 'recent' generally means a month or two. This will give you a good idea what the market is dictating. The asking price and selling price can be different so it is important to know where the market is pointing.

From time to time, I also look at similar properties that were recently on the market but didn't sell. If these properties are priced above market values then they can serve as good examples for a seller who leans towards overpricing a property. Otherwise, it is difficult to determine the reason for not selling and I don't always use this segment for the CMA.

At this point, I have a price range that is appropriate for this property. I continue with the second part of my process.

The Context of Selected Properties (Step 2)

In the CMA, I have chosen the properties to be included. The second step is to show you the context of these selected properties.

For the current properties that I used, i.e. the properties that your home will be competing with, I went to the MLS® listings and printed a total of approximately 15-20 properties (4 per page) that are lower, similar and higher in price.

I lay these pages in front of you with the selected properties circled in red. We then discuss the price range resulting from the CMA and see where that fits among these properties.

We take a few moments and study some of the specifications of these homes. We review the higher priced ones and make a decision as to whether or not a lower price is reasonable for your home. Similarly, we look at the lower priced ones and determine that your home has better features and should be priced above those. We are now satisfied that the price range is appropriate.

I have a similar set for properties recently sold and we also review those in a like manner.

Now that you have seen the information and agree with the price range, I ask you to actually pick the asking price.

Seller Picks Listing Price

Most REALTORS® present a completed CMA with a suggested list price.

I have always built my CMA by starting with the second step to make my selections for the CMA. In my experience, showing the seller how I arrived at those selections brings clarity to the seller. The seller can see that these are not arbitrary selections and he begins to build confidence in the price range.

This is not a scientific process. It consists of skill and experience which produces a reasonable range of values. Within that range, a price has to be selected to facilitate the MLS® System.

Now that the seller has a good understanding, I ask him what the list price should be. Reflecting on our previous discussions, he determines if he wishes to be near the top or bottom of the price range or somewhere in the middle. After a moment or two, there is generally a smile and a list price.

Advantages of Step 2 Process

The biggest advantage has been that the seller takes **ownership** of the asking price. He has seen how it is built, understands it and was a participant in the price selection.

If the market changes and a price reduction is appropriate, this process simplifies a price reduction.

There are other advantages for the seller.

For example, as REALTORS® we often state that the market dictates price not us. For the most part that is true. However, in a closed community such as a condo building, townhouse complex or mobile home park, a well-known REALTOR® in that community can affect pricing. By pricing a property too low, the resulting sale becomes a barometer for other listings and sales. As a result, if the REALTOR® continues this process, property values can go down in that closed community even though elsewhere that is not the case.

When I list a property in a closed community and see an abnormally low sale price, I don't include it until I find out the reason. If it is a distress sale or if there is some other reason for a quick sale, it is not a legitimate property to include in a CMA because it was not affected by market conditions. Such a sale is due to personal circumstances and not market conditions.

The seller should be aware that it is the responsibility of the REALTOR®, when working on behalf of the seller, to obtain the best price possible for the client. Your REALTOR® can provide you with all the necessary information you need to help you make a good pricing decision. This may be particularly important for sellers in closed communities such as condos, townhouse complexes and mobile home parks.

Marketing

Now that I have all the information and we established a price, I discuss how I will provide the necessary exposure and appeal to potential buyers so that they will know this home is for sale and interest them enough to view it and possibly make an offer to purchase. In other words -- How will I market your property?

There are many avenues and I'll cover the most frequently used techniques.

The Sign

Placing a sign on the property seems like a very basic thing to do. You list your property and the REALTOR® places a sign on your lawn.

Some buyers drive around neighbourhoods they like so they can see what is for sale. According to surveys, 12%-15% of buyers have located their new home through real estate signs on the property. (See Appendix A)

If you choose not to have one, you are missing opportunities to sell.

The Lock Box

I mention this as a marketing technique because accessibility is vital. It doesn't matter how much marketing I do, if this is not accompanied my accessibility, it will hinder selling opportunities.

New technologies applied to lock boxes make them highly sturdy and, therefore, much safer than in previous decades. Many can also be programmed so that entry can only take place between certain hours. This provides peace of mind to those who are apprehensive about lock boxes and feel that entry might take place in the middle of the night. As REALTORS®, we sometimes work long hours but definitely avoid midnight showings!

For safety reasons, in many regions, these lock boxes have to be updated on a daily basis. We use a code to gain access - so even if someone managed to find out the code, it would expire by day's end.

One more point worthy of note. These electronic marvels also keep a record of which REALTOR® entered, on which day and at what time.

Where possible, allow a lock box. Sometimes it is more difficult with properties that have tenants. Notice has to be given to tenants prior to showings and days and hours may be restricted to accommodate them.

Listing on MLS® System

A REALTOR® really has 2 options when listing -- MLS® System or Exclusive.

I wouldn't even think of listing a property 'exclusive'. It used to be more popular at one time but the reason escapes me. What 'exclusive' means is that only the listing REALTOR® has the right to sell the property and the property's exposure is limited to what this REALTOR® does. Bottom line, with an 'exclusive' listing, fewer people are aware of the property's existence.

However, listing on the MLS® System provides the greatest exposure -- greater than any other vehicle available anywhere. The system is financed by REALTORS® who pay a fee for each listing and/or pay via a monthly fee.

Each real estate board has a facility whereby REALTORS® can access and view daily listings that come onto the market place. Very handy when you are working with buyers and need the most up-to-date information.

MLS® System is the best system for anyone looking for property in Canada. It can be accessed through www.realtor.ca. South of the border they use www.realtor.com

The buyers' survey (Appendix A) indicates that buyers are using the MLS® System more and more. Back in 2005 it was about 20% and this has steadily risen where in 2008 it was approaching 30%. Almost 30% of buyers first locate their property by checking MLS® listings on www.realtor.ca.

Locating Homes Through REALTORS®

This is the major way that home buyers locate properties - through REALTORS®! According to the buyers' survey (Appendix A), the range is between 35%-40% over the 4 year period. If you add in the MLS® System, the 2008 figures indicate that over 60% of buyers locate their properties in this fashion.

Such statistics suggest that REALTORS® are a very effective group of professionals. We have the best systems in place which we financially support. And, we cooperate with each other to provide the best client service and information.

When we are working with buyers - we are very in tune with the market place. We check new MLS® listings on a daily basis to see if anything comes on the market that meets the buyers' needs.

During our office meetings, REALTORS® inform us of any new listings they have or about to have. We also discuss what some of our buyers' are looking for to see if anyone is about to list such a property.

Some REALTORS® use web service providers that email new listings to all of us highlighting features of the property.

As REALTORS®, we rarely miss an opportunity to promote our clients' properties.

Personal Internet Sites

Many of us have invested in our own websites. Generally, there is a direct link from the properties you find on the MLS® System to the listing REALTOR'S® web site where you may find more information.

These stand alone sites provide additional property exposure. Sometimes consumers search via different criteria to find properties. If your website contains these criteria, it would rise to the surface.

I currently have two residential real estate sites. Google my name and they will appear.

Real Estate Corporate Sites

Many large franchise real estate companies have invested in their own websites. Often they are quite elaborate BUT the consumer is limited because these sites only showcase those companies' listings.

As a consumer, I would like to see all listed properties before making any viewing or purchasing decisions.

Nevertheless, it does provide additional exposure for properties listed by these companies.

Real Estate Tabloids and Classifieds

This is generally local print advertising. Referring to the buyers' survey (at back of book), buyers don't often locate their properties through these avenues - under 5%. However, when buyers first think of purchasing, they often browse through these publications.

Open House

Again, this is another way of exposing your home. Despite many changes in the industry, some REALTORS® continue to do Open Houses. It still seems to be a staple in the industry.

A much more detailed discussion appears later in this book.

Office Tour

Office Tours are traditional in most regions. It consists of local REALTORS® doing a quick tour of newly listed properties. Not all regions conduct their office tours in the same manner. Some are better than others. Nevertheless, this is an option that is open for you.

I discuss this in greater detail in the section entitled 'Office Tour'.

Paperwork

Now that we have looked at the market place, established price and discussed marketing strategies, it is time to start the paperwork.

Agency Relationship - "Working with a REALTOR®"

It begins with agency relationship which has been described at the outset.

Individual Identification Information Record

This is also known as FINTRAC and has also been described in the earlier part of the book.

Multiple Listing Contract

I have already completed some information such as name address and legal description that I was aware of and confirm this with you.

Length of Contract

We then establish the length of this contract. This may vary from 60 days and up. It depends on the market situation, the property and its location. For example, rural properties, homes with unique features, acreages and so on will take longer than a 3 bedroom home in town.

List Price

I enter the list price as discussed.

Listing Brokerage Fee

Here I insert the dollar amount or the percentage of the selling price which my Brokerage will receive. Upon the sale, I receive a portion of this as per my contract with my Brokerage. The Selling Brokerage will also receive a respectable portion of the total fee collected.

There are no standard, fixed or average rates within the industry. It is against the Competition Act to discuss or fix rates among real estate companies.

My rate reflects my experience, my service, the type of property, location, length of marketing, cost of marketing and many 'overhead' factors -- license fees, Errors & Omission Insurance, board fees, office fees, internet fees, equipment and so on.

My real estate business is a quality full service business. I want to provide my clients with the best opportunity not only to sell their properties but to get the best possible prices. To that end, I take advantage of all appropriate marketing opportunities, remain in touch and available to my clients and provide a respectable real estate fee to attract selling brokerages.

When I review and complete the listing contract, we all sign and date it.

Property Disclosure

This document is completed by you, the seller. It provides the potential buyer with information about your property. It is based on your actual knowledge, to the best of your knowledge.

When agreed to by buyer and seller, it becomes part of the purchase contract.

Residential Data Input

This form contains all the property information for the listing including square footage, room sizes, legal description, appointment notes and so on.

Measuring Home

The data input form requires the square footage of the home and room measurements. I use an electronic gadget to measure most of the rooms. Sometimes a room doesn't lend itself to electronics and I have to measure by hand. I also measure the outside, draw a diagram of the house and insert my measurements to obtain the square footage.

I can actually hire a service to do this and often I do. However, sometimes it is more expedient to be able to complete the entire listing sooner than later so I do it myself. I also find it beneficial since it familiarizes me with the home even more. Walking and measuring the outside often leads to further observations and sometimes even questions. It is always good to know as much as possible about the property.

Photos

The last thing I do is take photos of the home and property. If the day is not suitable for a complete set because of inadequate lighting or weather, I still take a few to start and return on a more suitable day for retakes.

Concluding Listing Appointment

I have all the information, I require including measurements and photos. I leave a copy of the contract with the sellers and return in a couple of days with a copy of the uploaded listing.

Before I leave, I place a For Sale sign on the property.

Examining Some Real Estate Traditions

Vi Brown

Open House

The MLS® Books

There was a time, not that long ago, when we didn't use computers and had to rely on MLS® books. These MLS® books were printed a couple of times a month and contained ONE black and white photo, the property address and description.

Consequently, REALTORS® incorporated Open Houses as part of their marketing plan. As soon as I listed a residential property, I automatically did an Open House or two. It was then also more common for potential buyers to make the rounds of Open Houses in their neighbourhoods of interest. After all, photocopies from the MLS® book didn't provide a very good visual of the property.

The Open House Experience

At that time, I had a plan for conducting an Open House. I would place an ad in the local paper advertising the Open House on a specific day and time. I would then create a beautiful feature sheet and bring along enough copies for a parade. I would arrive early and put out ample signage to the property. When I arrived, the sellers were either already gone or on their way. I would check through the house - open all room doors and put on all the lights. Sometimes I noted that the sellers left jewellery or change on dressers, expensive cameras and other valuable items were around the house but I thought it would be safe since I would be accompanying the Open House visitors.

In some popular neighbourhoods it was not uncommon to have twenty-five or more groups of people come through my Open House. Usually there were at least two people in a group but sometimes they came with children, other relatives or friends.

It was fine when all these visitors were spread out over the two-hour period. I could escort each group through the house. That, however, was not the case. Sometimes there was no one there for 30 minutes and then two or 3 groups appeared at once. They knew the protocol - remove shoes, pick up a feature sheet and check out the home. Some would go one way, others would head upstairs and sometimes the parents allowed their children to explore on their own. I usually ended up following the children and tried to get them back to their parents, but not always successfully.

When I first started doing Open Houses, some of them were out of control. Too many people arriving at one time and not enough me. I felt responsible for what took place at my Open Houses while under my watch. I have paid for broken toys that enthusiastic visiting children fought over and broke. I recovered items that were inadvertently going out the front door. Busy Open Houses caused me enough anxiety that I finally developed a way to control them.

Since Open Houses were part of the marketing package for residential properties, I also did Open Houses in rural homes. There is always a smaller market for rural properties and so the attendance at an Open House was rather slim -- sometimes no one appeared. It was so quiet. How quiet was it? So quiet that I could fall asleep!

I was once doing an Open House in a newer subdivision when I received a call on my cell from a fellow REALTOR® who was also doing one on the next street. She advised me that a lone man was suspiciously walking around the neighbourhood and that I should not let him in to the Open House if I was there alone. He had entered her Open House but saw that there were others present so he wandered around outside. As her visitors were leaving, he approached but she quickly stated that the Open House was closed and locked the door. This man was now headed in my direction. Just as she was telling me, I saw a man heading up the path. I quickly locked the door and headed to the back door to lock it as well. He appeared in the back yard. I suggested that my colleague call the police and I was going to warn another REALTOR® working in the area. The police caught up with this man and questioned him but could do nothing as he didn't break any laws. Open Houses were for the public and he wanted to see these homes.

I did many Open Houses in the earlier years because that was a marketing tool that we had by which we could showcase the home. I did Open Houses in old houses, new houses, country houses, condos, townhouses and mobiles. In all those years, I never sold a house that I could directly attribute to an Open House. I did, however, meet buyers at Open Houses who became clients and to whom I sold homes.

The Impact of the Internet

Now, real estate is on the internet! Whichever site you visit to search for real estate properties, you will find ample coloured photos as well as virtual tours. The largest site that carries all listed properties and is financed and kept up to date by the real estate membership is www.realtor.ca.

More and more buyers are searching the web. Before ever contacting a REALTOR® and going to see the home, many buyers already have a good idea of what the property looks like. Inside and outside photos provide a potential buyer with the flavour of each home that is of interest.

Why do REALTORS® Still do Open Houses?

I have asked some of my colleagues why they continue to do Open Houses. The most common response is that their sellers want at least one Open House during the term of the listing. If the home does not generate enough interest, the answer seems to be to do more Open Houses.

Many REALTORS® still make an Open House a regular part of their marketing process. That would be reasonable if houses actually sold at Open Houses -- but they don't. In annual surveys done from 2005 to 2008 (see Appendix A), buyers indicate how they have located their properties. About 40% of buyers locate properties through REALTORS®, almost 30% find their properties on www.realtor.ca and even a real estate sign is responsible for about 12%. Open Houses are at the bottom of the list (under 2%) with classified ads (under 1%).

Please check Appendix A at the back of this book.

Are Open Houses Productive?

In my opinion, Open Houses are not productive. On a nice sunny afternoon, many people spend part of their day going to Open Houses. For some, it is an afternoon's entertainment. Others like to get decorating ideas. Neighbours are curious and like to drop in for a look.

Those who are planning a purchase 'next year' may also go to Open Houses. Sometimes it is difficult to determine even why someone has come to an Open House. And yes, sometimes a true buyer, that is, a buyer who is ready purchase, drops in as well. Such a buyer is usually working with a REALTOR® but on this day, he has decided to explore the neighbourhood and came upon this Open House. If this potential buyer is interested, his REALTOR® will make an appointment for a more detailed viewing. A REALTOR® would not be doing his due diligence if he were to write an offer without actually seeing the property himself.

On a rainy day, Open Houses are lightly attended, if at all. On those days, the REALTOR® spends some quiet time in the sellers' home. There is also minimal attendance at Open Houses in condos, mobile homes as well as rural properties.

Getting Serious about Open Houses

Today, serious buyers don't run all over town to attend Open Houses to make their home purchase selection. They browse the internet and/or they contact a REALTOR®, discuss their wants, review computer generated listings with descriptions and photos. Select those that they wish to see and their REALTOR® then sets up appointments to view these properties.

An Open House means that you, the seller, are inviting strangers into your home and you are not even there. We don't pick up strangers in our cars but we allow strangers to walk through our homes.

With today's technology, the Open House concept, in most instances, is an obsolete marketing tool. It doesn't sell homes -- it poses a risk to the sellers' property -- it can place the REALTORS® at risk -- and it takes time away from the REALTORS'® families since most Open Houses take place on the weekends. In applying the cost/benefit analysis to an Open House, it seems that the possible cost far outweighs the likelihood of a benefit.

In effect, the Open House is truly the dinosaur of real estate. But, that is only my opinion. Sellers can decide.

More Views on Open Houses

If I do an Open House at the specific request of my seller, it is a controlled Open House. My usual instructions to the seller are to put away valuables and not leave jewellery, watches, money and the like easily accessible. And, do not leave your medications on your night table. For that matter, don't even leave them in your bathroom medicine cabinet. These items appear to have increased in interest.

There are other valuables in a home like small pieces of art work, carvings, figurines which sellers don't think of putting away safely. I have accessed the seller's home and I am responsible for what occurs there. I do not wish to be responsible for lost property or damage done by visitors under my watch. Nor do I wish my seller's privacy to be invaded by visitors checking items that are not for sale such as dresser drawers and so on.

To control an Open House, I generally invite a friend or perhaps a new REALTOR® to join me. Someone who is not licensed in real estate is not permitted to provide information about properties as per our regulations. So the friend serves only as a safety and control factor while a new REALTOR® can actually assist in providing property information and at the same time gain Open House experience.

Here is my procedure at an Open House. I have a sign in guest book requiring visitors' name, address and phone number so that I have a record of who entered the seller's home. Very rarely does anyone refuse and if they do, I don't allow them through the home. Some visitors ask that their phone numbers not be used to follow up to which I agree. Some REALTORS® collect contact information at Open Houses to see if they can be of assistance to some of these visitors in purchasing a home. The incentive for a new REALTOR® to assist me in my Open House is the opportunity to possibly make contact with some of the visitors that appear at the Open House.

Once the guests have signed in and I've provided them with an information sheet on the property, I escort them through the house and answer their questions. If others come in during that time, the friend who has accompanied me, will ask them to wait a few moments till I return. If I have a new REALTOR® with me, he/she can provide property information while waiting for me to complete my tour and then can proceed with the other visitors. If small children join their parents through an Open House, I ask that they keep their children with them so that they don't run from room to room.

Having turned on all the lights and opened all doors at the beginning of the Open House, at the end, I ensure that everything is returned to normal and all lights are turned off. The next day I provide feedback to the sellers.

Two people present at an Open House create a much safer environment for the REALTOR® and allow for greater care of the sellers' home and possessions.

Productive Open Houses

There are times when Open Houses are useful.

New Construction -- In a development, the contractor generally completes one building to showcase the rest of the development. It is attractively 'staged' with furnishings and decorative lighting. Sometimes even the landscaping is completed surrounding this show piece. In most instances, there is a daily Open House during the remaining construction phase. Potential buyers who are interested in this development have an opportunity to view an example of homes to come.

Fast Market -- There are times in a quick moving sellers' market, that an Open House may be productive for the seller. When buyers are competing for listed homes in the market place, an astute REALTOR® may do an Open House rather than set up separate appointments and stipulate that all offers should be presented at a specific time later that same afternoon. This could create a multiple offer situation whereby the seller may receive an offer above the listed price. The listing REALTOR®, working on behalf of his sellers, is maximizing the opportunity to obtain the best possible price for his client, the seller, through the Open House.

The Office Tour

Almost the same argument can be made regarding office tours as with Open Houses. When I check for new entries on the market, I access my board's MLS® System and can get a good idea of the properties through the many photos that are posted. Of what benefit is the office tour to the seller?

Productive Office Tour

When I first came to the west coast, I found the manner in which this community conducted office tours was very productive for REALTORS® and sellers.

Let me briefly explain how they were organized. There were three major real estate offices and one or two smaller ones for a total of about 100 real estate agents. Every Monday at 9:00 am, all the offices held their office meetings. Immediately after, we all went on tour. We were strongly advised to come to the office meetings and, therefore, many REALTORS® were available for the tour.

Between 10:00 am and noon, the listing REALTORS® were stationed in the homes that they had on tour. The doors were open, the lights were on, information was available, special features were pointed out and so on. Some offered snacks, others offered a draw for a bottle of wine and occasionally there would be a light lunch available. These were some of the ways of enticing as many REALTORS® as possible to tour the home.

REALTORS® were able to tour all the homes or, if pressed for time, select those that were of greatest interest to buyers they had. During that two-hour period, you had the opportunity to spend some time in the homes, ask the REALTOR® questions about the property and get a good sense of each home and the pricing.

Because it was a smaller town, the Office Tour provided an opportunity for the REALTORS® to be familiar with everything in that market place. When I had a buyer moving into the area, I knew virtually every property available. I knew if it needed some work or was ready to move into. I knew if it had a large yard or small yard. I could listen to my buyer's requirements and pick out the appropriate homes.

From the seller's point of view, it was equally productive. The REALTORS® who came on the tour had sufficient time to become familiar with the property and to be aware of some of the specifics. Many of us noted some home features on our tour sheets and made notes regarding which buyers might be interested. It was not unusual for requests for showings to take place after office tours. I know that I often had calls from REALTORS® after a tour who wanted to set up appointments for their clients.

When the listing REALTOR® asked for input regarding price on a more unusual property, he got it. These REALTORS® took that bit of extra time to assess, based on their current experience of what was on the market, and wrote their recommended list price on the back of their business cards - often with a comment or two. These were often discussed with the sellers.

An Office Tour, in that community, was a highly effective marketing tool. The majority of REALTORS® used it.

Unproductive Tours

Having experienced the previous style of Office Tours, the 'caravan' type of tour, for me is unproductive.

This kind of tour involves REALTORS® following each other in 'caravan' style. The listing REALTOR® is among them rushing to be ahead of everyone a moment or two so that he can open the door of the home on tour. Everyone removes shoes, goes through the home and is back out in a couple of moments putting on shoes. You get back in the car and follow the 'caravan' to the next stop where another REALTOR® opens the home for a quick walk through by their fellow colleagues. In the meantime, the first REALTOR® may be too late for the second stop so rushes to catch up at the third stop. I'm sure you get the idea.

After having attended such tours several times, I observed that I couldn't remember much about any of the homes I rushed through! There was no time to really view anything.

Yet, under these circumstances, REALTORS® were sometimes asked to give their opinions regarding the property. I have seen some of these comments on the back of business cards - "Too high" - "Very Nice" - "Nice View" - "Reduce Price".

I certainly couldn't give an opinion. I didn't see enough. And the comments that were provided were not of any use to the listing REALTOR® or the seller.

In some areas, that is the only kind of office tour that is available. Perhaps it can be made more productive with a few changes. It's the seller's decision if they wish an office tour.

Your Home Stager

Josée Lalonde

A Little about Me

Josée Lalonde is a native of Ottawa, Ontario. Even from her crib, ever observant, Josée would think -

"Why? Why? Why! Why aren't my crib bumpers and my little sheets matching?"

"How come the drapes and window coverings aren't complementing the cushions on my little rocking chair?"

As far back as she can remember, Josée has harboured a talent that needed to be explored and shared!

OK, that was my husband's version!

The fact is, even in my early teens, I was hooked on room design. My parents supported my muse by giving me 'carte blanche' to reorganize my bedroom however I pleased. Little did they know that I would redesign the entire space!

Thankfully, they got over the shock and continued to support my creative streak. I was free to roll with my ideas. Best of all, my 'one of a kind' bedroom became the envy of all my friends. I had found my gift. But that was long before there was even such a thing as 'home staging'.

In 1995, I graduated from my 'Soins Dentaires' course at La Cité Collegiale and became a certified dental assistant, a career I have genuinely loved.

The first clinic in which I worked was a bit 'dated', to be polite. The office was changing hands and a younger dentist was taking over. This was the perfect opportunity to volunteer my creative skills and give the space the 'update' it needed. With a tiny budget, I went for it -- my first successful makeover! My passion grew!

My many years as a dental assistant has served to further develop my organizational skills, time management and efficiency. These traits have become invaluable in my career as a home stager and designer.

In 2006, my husband's career brought us to Victoria in beautiful British Columbia. New roots, a new chapter, and the opportunity to embark on the career I have always dreamed about.

To that end, I completed studies in home staging in Vancouver in 2007. I was now certified as a Canadian Staging Professional. I was finally 'legit'! It was time to take my passion for staging and design to a new level.

My business is entitled 'Josée Lalonde Real Estate Staging' and can be found on www.joseelalonde.ca. My website contains before and after photos of homes that I have staged. In many instances, I entered the process after the homes had been on the market for months. Virtually all of them sold within weeks, if not days, after being staged. You can also read testimonials I received for my work by both clients and REALTORS®.

As my business continues to grow, so does my passion for it.

Home Staging

"Cost is the excuse. Desire is the obstacle."

A History

We are a little behind the eight ball in North America with this seemingly 'new' concept called 'Home Staging'. The fact is that in several European countries, back in the early 1850's, 'presenting' a home for sale was already recognized as an important step in the process of transferring ownership.

More recently, in 1972, Barb Schwartz, a real estate agent in the United States, realized that there was something missing, some key element, something that would ensure a quick and profitable sale. With a background in design, she began to put more emphasis on making one of her listed properties more presentable and, voila! She discovered the key she had been looking for -- most potential buyers truly need help to be able to see the value of a property.

So, although Barb Schwartz may have been the first to coin the term 'staging', the techniques have been practiced on the other side of the Atlantic for well over 100 years. One thing we know for sure is that since it hit North American shores, the trend of home staging as an aid to selling a property, has grown phenomenally. And thanks to the ever-increasing popularity of specialty television networks like HGTV (Home and Garden Television); 'home staging' has become the buzz word on everyone's lips these days.

Definition

But what exactly *is* Home Staging? In a nut shell, home staging can be defined as the technical art of preparing a property for sale which, in return, will result in the highest possible selling price for the owner in the shortest time frame. With a trained and objective eye, the home stager uses techniques that are known to showcase the best features of a property while simultaneously downplaying its flaws.

Hiring a Professional Home Stager

> *"Nothing changes until something moves."*
> -Albert Einstein

Why Home Staging?

When it comes to purchasing a home, the potential buyer must make an emotional connection to that property the moment he or she first sees the home and walks through its front door. The old adage that you only have one chance to make a good first impression was never truer than when real estate is presented to the buying market.

Independent surveys show that, once a prospective buyer enters a home, of all the factors that impact on a buyer's decision to buy, only 28% are out of the control of the seller. This refers to such things as the number of rooms and the floor plan. The remaining 72% of the factors that determine whether or not a buyer will place an offer to purchase are *within the control of the seller*. Cleanliness, odour, degree of clutter – it all counts. Lighting and décor alone account for over one half of weighted factors that influence the buyer. This is why the advice and talents of a professional home stager are so important.

Who Refers to a Home Stager?

There are basically three sources of referrals to the home stager; the real estate agent, the property developer, and the home owner.

The Real Estate Agent

It is the truly savvy real estate agent that insists on staging a property before listing it for sale. They know, firsthand, about the win-win-win relationship that staging could offer to the process of selling a property in the market place. A 'staged' home may sell quicker and for more money resulting in a satisfied seller, happy real estate agent and a busy and successful home stager. This is Win-Win-Win! Your real estate agent can certainly refer you to an enthusiastic and experienced home stager.

The Property Developer

For condominium buildings, as for single homes in a development project, the property developer will usually opt for staging one or more 'show suites', to give the property a bit of warmth and a sense of dimension and space. The benefit here, of course, is that staging a single unit serves as the showcase for all similar units.

The Homeowner

The word is out. More and more homeowners have become aware of the benefits of staging the property they wish to sell. It has become increasingly common for the homeowner to begin working with a home stager, even before contacting or listing with their real estate agent. They know that if the property is listed and photographed *before* it is staged, they risk the disappointment of having it sit on the market for too long. The property will have already been viewed (and rejected) by the first, and most important, wave of potential buyers. These 'buyers', like 85% of the population, are simply not able to see the full property value if it is not properly staged.

The Staging Process: From Consultation to Open House!

*"One of the great disadvantages of hurry
is that it takes such a long time."*
-G. K. Chesterton

The Consultation Report

Once the home stager has had the opportunity to go through and thoroughly photograph the property, they can get on with the business of preparing a report for the client to review and consider. The nature of the report depends on the size and nature of the property being staged, the desires and limitations of the client, and the amount of furniture, art, and accessories required for the job.

Let me use an example of how I go about the initial meeting: After I've introduced myself, I ask the client to kindly walk through the house with me. After we have gone through every room, I let the client go back to what they were doing, or give them my photo portfolio to look through. That leaves me free to take photographs and make some notes. For me, this is where my ideas start to germinate as to what work will need to be done to the property to make it more saleable. In my head, I can start to arrange the steps that must occur to take it to that point, starting from how it looks right now. When I am satisfied that I have all the information I need, I again sit down with the homeowner.

At this stage, I establish the kind of budget the homeowner has for staging and give them a rough idea of the process as it relates to their specific property. I also include what they can expect to receive from me by way of a report and a ballpark quote. With experience, the home stager is able to provide a reasonably accurate estimate of most jobs.

Back at my office, I will prepare a comprehensive report and a proposal that I strive to deliver within two days following the consultation. This takes considerable time since the report details all the information necessary to prepare each room before it can actually be staged. Then the client can decide whether or not they want to follow through with the staging.

Basically, there are three major types of reports:

1) Lived-In property consultation with fine tuning:

This is the "Do It Yourself" approach to home staging. If the owner has most of the right furnishings, artwork and accessories, the home stager simply provides a report that details what it is the client should do to get their house ready to sell. This will include recommended de-cluttering, temporary storage of unnecessary items and perhaps even minor renovations (painting, flooring, minor repairs, etc.). The client is on their own to follow through with the recommendations. If the client wishes, the home stager may return to the property for a few hours to help 'fine tune' their efforts before the house finally goes on the market.

2) Lived-In property consultation in preparation for staging (showcasing):

In these cases, the home is furnished but needs some editing and some additional furnishings and accessories that the home stager will select, or 'source out'. As above, the report will start by advising the client on exactly what *they* need to do to ready the house. It will also include a rough estimate of what items are needed for what rooms and an estimate of the expected costs. A list of contacts can be provided of tradesmen who may be able to assist the owner, if needed. When that work is completed, the home stager can then come back to the property to do what they do best!

3) Vacant property consultation in preparation for staging (showcasing):

In the case of vacant properties, we have the opportunity to work from a blank slate. Some properties might require minor renovations or repairs and this will be included in the written report, same as above. If the property doesn't require any renovation-type changes, there will be no written report but simply a proposal for the rentals of furnishings, accessories and artwork.

Scheduling

Ideally, showcasing should be done *before* a property is listed for sale. According to a recent study, 77% of buyers will first view the listings on MLS®, meaning that the pictures have to be perfect to get the potential buyers' initial interest. The more time a seller has to prepare the property, the better, but we all know that time is not always on our side and deadlines are inevitable. A lot of factors can come into play; time for the client to accomplish what they need to do, time for the stager to source out for specific items, furniture rentals, furniture delivery schedules, stagers' schedules, etc. From my experience, between five to seven days from the date staging can begin is a reasonable time period to allow before committing to photographing and listing a property.

We also need to be respectful of the other professionals who may be involved with the project. Real estate agents maintain lists of clients looking to purchase certain types of properties. Of course, the sooner a property can be listed and an Open House scheduled, the sooner these buyers can see the property and put in an offer. Every real estate agent strives to get their sign on the property as soon as possible – it's just good advertising. The problem with this is that even a savvy real estate investor may have trouble seeing a property's true value if it is not suitably displayed. Taking everything into account, it is the seller who is in charge, and who must decide what schedule is best for them and what compromises need to be made. Once they've made their decisions, contracts can be signed, and the home stager can bring on their part of the magic!

Staging

So, the big day arrives and everything is ready to go. The homeowners have done their homework and the house is ready to be properly staged. I require free access to the house so the homeowners need to trust in their home stager to maintain a key or codes to the property; it gives flexibility for our ins and outs so we can be more time efficient.

I also request (more like "insist") that the homeowners (and their pets) are out of the house while staging is ongoing. This is important for several reasons.

First, we have a 'game plan' and we cannot afford any interruptions. We have a lot to do and we usually have a deadline to meet which can sometimes be very tight. I can recall one project we did. Things were progressing well and although we were close to finishing, we thought we still had a couple of hours left to fine-tune. However, because of a miscommunication, the real estate agent showed up saying he was there to prepare for his Open House... that was to start in 15 minutes! We must have looked like we were in a silent movie, running around like madmen! That was way too tight!

Second, from this point on, the house needs to be considered more as a 'product', and less as a 'home'. What we need to accomplish to make it saleable may not always suit the owners' own sense of style and it can be hard to 'let it go' at first. Rest assured the home stager truly understands how difficult this process can be; to let go of those lived in memories. However, we must keep in mind that the process is one of 'moving on' to the next chapter of our lives, where new memories will be built. Needless to say, things can go so much easier if the owner is out of the house. And, in the end, the homeowner is always amazed and excited with the results.

Finally, when we are in the midst of staging, the place will always look worse before it looks better. When we are 'mid-project', it can look like a bomb went off, which can be a little overwhelming even for the stager. The less the client sees of that, the better!

Pre-Open House Inspection

Not everybody offers this step but I believe it makes a real difference, especially if the Open House is a week or more away from when the staging was finished. If the property is still 'lived-in', it can be too much to expect the owners to maintain it *exactly* how we left it. An hour or two before the Open House, I like to pay a visit to the property to do a little 'tweaking' -- a last minute inspection for a great first impression!

A Note about the Exterior

Curb appeal is a crucial factor in preparing a home. Research shows that 74% of potential buyers will 'just drive by' the house before deciding if they are going to bother making an appointment to view the inside of the property. Part of the rationale for that is so a potential buyer can get a feel for the neighbourhood and the surrounding amenities, but part of it is also to get a look at the exterior aesthetics. There is no sense transforming the interior of a home into a buyer's dream if we can't get the potential buyer to walk through the front door.

Degrees of Home Staging

"Compromise is alright, as long as your values don't change."
-Jane Goodall

There are always options or different degrees of home staging available to the client. Unless otherwise discussed and agreed to, my proposal is presented to include staging of the entire house. However, budgets are a fact of life and we must try our very best to work within them. Addressing the whole house would be the ideal, but it is possible to focus on certain areas of the home to take advantage of the features that we feel will make the greatest difference.

Staging 'Key' Rooms

It is essential to stage the most fundamental rooms of a house. Imagine a clean, nice smelling, spacious kitchen that beckons you to 'come, entertain, and cook!' Or a living or family room that is so inviting you just want to curl up on the couch, maybe by the fireplace, and read a book or watch a great movie. How about a master bedroom that is so heavenly you just want to lie on the bed and fall into a deep sleep, after having taken a wonderful relaxing bath in the spa-like ensuite bathroom…see what I mean? There are certain rooms that are essential, or 'key', to stage for a house to sell successfully. In a way, we are trying to sell a lifestyle. People need to feel like they belong. They can see themselves living there. The key rooms are those that potential buyers will be spending most of their valuable time enjoying life, entertaining, and relaxing. Lifestyle!

Staging of Specific Floors

The fact is, the potential buyer takes only three to six minutes to visit a house the first time. That means that, as they walk in, they decide almost instantly if it's going to be a keeper. Will they be back for another look? We never get a second chance to make a first impression, so the main entrance is really the most important. If the budget permits, we can also stage the second floor, or perhaps a finished basement. Many homes these days have 'in-law' or rental suites. These suites are just as important as a main floor because they are usually smaller and have odd angles that challenge even the talents of an experienced pro. By showcasing it to reveal its full potential and space, we can add greater value to the property.

Staging of Specific Rooms

On an even tighter budget, we may be able to prepare only certain rooms, those that require staging the most. For example, empty rooms, rooms that need to return to their original purpose (office space back to a bedroom). Rooms that are too cluttered should be staged to help the potential buyer recognize better value. It's not uncommon for these rooms to be on separate floors. We may need to do a couple of rooms per floor… whatever works best with the given budget.

Consultation Only – No Staging

Respectfully, there are clients that have virtually no budget. In these cases, the client simply pays the consultation fee (approximately $200-$300) and we prepare their consultation report that details what they can do on their own to optimize the presentation of their property.

Staging the entire house is ideal, but not always budget friendly for every client. By making a few wise compromises, anybody, big budget or small, can benefit from home staging.

The Full Meal Deal

Home staging doesn't have to stop at accessorizing and furniture placement, it also can include recommendations for minor renovations, painting, flooring, lighting changes, etc. These suggestions are usually included in the consult report, particularly if a minor effort will reap big returns. If the budget is not an issue, and we are given the time, we can go as far as you want to maximize a property's value.

Other Services

There are many other services that the home stagers can offer to their clients:

Organizing

Sometimes life gives you more than you can handle and certain priorities may have to take a back seat. The prospect of organizing a badly disorganized space can get a little overwhelming. Getting direction and a helping hand from an objective third party to help can save an enormous amount of time and grief. (One small catch... you have to keep it up!)

Staging for Living

'Staging' a space that is not necessarily for sale is becoming increasingly popular. This service leans more towards decorating or design but still fits comfortably under the umbrella of staging. As we do in a showcasing for sale, we can help you choose paint colors, flooring, lighting, etc. We can help you edit or add furnishings and accessories that will suit, all the while following the technical rules of staging to take advantage of the space. When finished, the homeowner can enjoy the benefits of a great stylish space for themselves. The bonus is, when it's time to sell, the property will already be market ready!

Move-In Staging

This service is similar to 'staging for living', just backwards! Let me use an example - we are recruited to stage a home that is going on the market. Using what the owners already have, and maybe adding some of our own inventory, the finished project is revealed to the client and they love it. As a consequence, they then hire us to 'stage' their new home! That is what I mean by 'backwards', we staged to sell, then staged to live!

Staging for Seniors

This is a fairly new concept in the world of staging but is growing in popularity. As stagers, we are able to help our elderly by providing them with proven techniques to help them transition to their next residence. They are usually faced with smaller living spaces like an in-law suite or seniors' home. Needless to say, they have to edit most of their belongings, which can be very difficult and unsettling for some. As an objective third party, we are able to make the transition much easier. As for the small living space, this is where the home stager really gets to shine. We can help create and maximize the space so that they can enjoy it to its fullest potential.

I was once hired to stage a newly renovated, vacant living space in a seniors' residence. It had to include a bedroom area, sitting area and eating area. The size -- only 200 square feet! This unit was not selling because, being vacant, nobody could imagine living in such a tiny space, let alone visualize how it could work as a comfortable living space. It was one of my biggest challenges, but still stands as one of my most rewarding projects.

Sourcing

As I mentioned before, this is one of my favourite services to provide. When you just can't find the time, the energy, or simply have no idea what you need to bring up the 'wow' factor of a property or single room, let an experienced and passionate expert do it for you. That is the thing about being passionate in my work. Whether consciously or unconsciously, I spend most of my waking hours (some of which I should be sleeping!) thinking about, and sourcing out products for staging. I probably already know what it is you need and where to find that special something. The advantage of this service is that you get to keep the item and use it in your next home!

Time and Money

"Price is what you pay, value is what you get."
-Warren Buffett

As mentioned in the 'scheduling' portion of this chapter, obviously the more time the better, but we do work with deadlines - they're just inevitable. Several factors can affect the timing of different projects. Is it a vacant house that needs to be fully furnished and accessorized? Is it a lived-in home that doesn't need much, maybe minimal items, some furniture rearranging? Is it a lived-in home that has an abundance of possessions that will need pre-packing and rental of a storage space? The length of time required will depend on the volume of work to be completed, the condition of the home and deadlines for other projects.

Fees are the biggest concern for clients, and rightly so. Everyone works hard for their money and there are lots of options for spending our disposable incomes. How much is it going to cost us for this service and what do I get out of it? Well, one thing is certain. While it is not easy to capture the exact return, it is normal for the cost of staging (at about 0.5-1% of the selling price) to result in a 3-5% higher selling price, relative to what it would have sold for (to say nothing about how much faster it will sell). Whatever the size of the project, consider home staging for sale as a very low-risk, high-return investment.

Basically, there are two approaches home stagers use when it comes to setting fees;

Hourly rate: The staging company charges an hourly rate for the project manager/lead stager and a separate hourly rate for the assistant(s). The stager will estimate the number of person-hours the project will take and charge accordingly.

Per square foot rate: The company will charge 'x' amount per square foot, say $0.35. It doesn't matter how long the staging process takes; it is the size of the rooms/house that determines the fees, much as if you were purchasing tiles, carpet or hardwood flooring.

The labour fees that we charge include several aspects that usually go unnoticed. They include our time for sourcing, planning, packing (accessories and such), travel time, actual staging (main stager and assistant), cleaning, and de-staging. The staging fee is a 'one time' charge. There are also rental fees for some of the furniture, accessories and artwork and these charges are paid on a monthly basis. Think of staging a home as 'an investment on an investment'. Without question, the cost will be less than your first price reduction.

Conclusion

The ultimate goal of Home Staging is to sell your house quicker and for more money by creating the ambiance of a lifestyle that potential buyers would want. In doing so, your property has an edge over others like it in the market place. However big or small the budget, there are options available to the home seller so that anyone can hire a home stager and be certain to get the greatest possible return on their investment. Home stagers can also offer other services, whether the homeowner is thinking of selling or just wishing to make staying a little longer feel fresher.

Time is always a factor but – let's face it - few of us are in a hurry to fail! In order to reap the full benefit of a staged home, it needs to be staged *before* it is listed. Proper staging is one of the best investments that can be made to maximize the equity in your house.

Finally, staging is but one of the ingredients in the recipe for selling a house. Others include asking price, location and physical condition. The price and the home's condition are under the control of the seller, the location is not. If the location and/or curb appeal does not attract the potential buyer, they will not bother to enter the home. But for those potential buyers for whom it is acceptable, the next step is to view the interior of the home. When they walk through the front door, they need to be 'blown away'.

A significant part of the recipe for the successful sale of a home is controlled by the seller, much of which is accomplished by the home stager. The time for selling a home is not the time to gamble.

Your Lawyer - for Seller

Kelly Orr

You Have Accepted Offer

This time you have decided to sell your home. You have worked with a real estate agent, have received a good offer which you have decided to accept. So what is your next step?

The good news is that with respect to the legal process, a sale is usually a much easier and less expensive proposition than a purchase. You first let your REALTOR® know that I will be representing you so that your REALTOR® can forward the accepted contract and any addenda to my office. I will review the documents to ascertain exactly what commitments you have been made, and what the buyer has agreed to pay and do, to ensure I can properly protect you.

Establishing Contact

Once I have received the documents from your REALTOR®, I will send a letter confirming that I have received instructions to act on your behalf and advising that, unless there are unusual circumstances, you probably will not hear from me further until it is time to sign documents. This will usually be within the last week prior to your sale (with the exception of contacting you for incidental matters such as whether you have a survey certificate that we could pass on to the buyer).

If you have any questions or concerns, however, I would encourage your calls as I want you to be comfortable with the entire sale process. Often selling a property and moving can be a very stressful experience and I would like to alleviate any stress that the legal process may cause you.

Charges on Title - Removable

My first task after receiving instructions will be to complete a search of your property to determine if there are financial encumbrances which need to be removed. Some of the charges we may need to remove are:

1. Mortgages are probably the most common charges that appear on a title. If you borrowed money to finance the purchase of your home or a subsequent renovation to your home, for instance, and secured the repayment of that loan by a mortgage, the money that you borrowed must be repaid so that we are able to compel the lender to provide us with a registrable discharge of the mortgage.

2. Builders Liens – If you have had work completed on your property there may be a Builders Lien against the title. In this case we will contact you to inquire about the circumstances. Perhaps the lien was filed because a contractor who worked for you did not pay a trade contractor or supplier. Perhaps a lien was filed by a contractor with whom you had a dispute as to the quality of the work. In any event, I will get to the bottom of why the lien was filed and either pay it out, negotiate a settlement or fight the lien and have it removed from title on your behalf.

3. Strata Property Act Liens – If you have any strata fees owing, whether regular monthly fees, or fines which were levied by your strata council for infractions against the bylaws or rules, the strata council may have filed a lien against your property. In this case (and even if there are fees owing but a lien has not been filed) we will be required to obtain from the Strata Corporation a Certificate of Full Payment and an Information Certificate.

    The Certificate of Full Payment must be filed by the solicitor for the buyer so the transaction cannot be completed without this document. The Strata Corporation will not provide the document unless and until all fees are paid (or unless I provide them with an undertaking to pay the fees out of the sale proceeds) and, accordingly, I will contact you to find out the circumstances behind the lien. If you have a dispute with the Strata Corporation, I will arrange to have funds held in trust pending settlement of the dispute. In any event, I will do what is necessary to obtain the Certificate of Full Payment to ensure we are able to proceed to completion.

4.   Judgments – If someone has sued you and obtained a judgment against you, the judgment may have been filed against your property and, in that case, I will have to contact the judgment holder and arrange for payout and discharge of the judgment.

In the majority of cases, the only charges I will need to worry about are mortgages. My next step, therefore, is to write to the mortgage lender and ask to be provided with a statement which sets out the amount of money the mortgage lender requires me to pay to compel them to sign and return to me a discharge of your mortgage. This amount of money will include the principal balance owing on the mortgage, any interest which will have accrued to and including the date scheduled for the payout, any discharge fee the lender might charge to provide us with a signed discharge of your mortgage, plus any penalty amount for an early repayment of the mortgage if such a penalty is applicable.

Normally if you repay your mortgage earlier than you are scheduled to, you will be required to pay a penalty. In most cases (although not all) the penalty will be either:

- an amount that is equal to three times the monthly amount of interest which is owing on your mortgage, or

- an interest differential amount. This amount is calculated by determining what interest rate the bank would charge to someone who wanted to take out a mortgage with a term equal to the term left on your mortgage. So, if you are paying your mortgage out 22 months early, the lender's closest term available would likely be two years. Accordingly, the lender would determine what their current interest rate is for a mortgage with a two year term. If that rate is less than what you are paying, the lender would calculate the difference and multiply that difference by the number of months left in your term.

For example, if you are paying 3.5% interest and the lender would charge 2.75% for a two year term mortgage, the difference would be 0.75%. The lender would calculate interest at 0.75% on the principal balance still owing on your mortgage over a period of 22 months.

The bank would compare the amounts calculated in each of the two previous paragraphs and would charge you whichever amount is greater.

The Legal Process

Reviewing Documents from Buyer's Lawyer

After I receive documents from the buyer's lawyer, I carefully examine them to make certain they conform to the details in the contract of purchase and sale that your REALTOR® provided to my office. In particular, I examine the Vendor's Statement of Adjustments to ensure you have received appropriate credit for items like the buyers' share of current property taxes, prepaid utilities or other prepaid expenses, and any additional items which the buyer may have agreed to pay you (for instance, for items such as wall hangings or garden equipment, which you have agreed to leave with the property). I further confirm that the math is correct and that the balance of sale proceeds the buyer's lawyer proposes to send us is the appropriate amount.

Preparing Documents

After confirming that the Vendor's Statement of Adjustments, prepared by the buyer's lawyer, is correct, and once I have received payout information regarding all financial encumbrances which we are required to remove from the title to your property, I will prepare an Order to Pay. This document starts with the balance of sale proceeds which the buyer's lawyer has agreed to send me (as indicated on the Vendor's Statement of Adjustments) and deducts the amounts I will be paying on your behalf such as real estate fees, mortgage payouts, outstanding utility levies, outstanding strata fees, legal fees and the like. The bottom line will be the balance of sale proceeds which will be paid to you (or applied to the purchase of another property, as the case may be).

Signing Documents

Once I have prepared the Order to Pay, I will contact you to set up an appointment for you to sign documents. When you attend at my office you will sign the following:

1. Our initial letter which is essentially some nagging reminders of items to be completed prior to moving out of your home (such as calling for utility meter readings, cancelling utility accounts, arranging for a mover to pack and move your possessions, cancelling your insurance coverage, and that sort of thing), along with approval of our estimated fees and disbursements;

2. A Form A Freehold Transfer

3. A GST/HST certificate (which will indicate that GST/HST is not payable on the sale price because the property is a used residential property that you did not build nor substantially renovate and that you have not claimed GST/HST input tax credits in relation to the property);

4. A residency certificate which states that you are a resident of Canada within the definitions set out in the Income Tax Act;

5. The Vendor's Statement of Adjustments; and

6. The Order to Pay.

We will discuss all the documents you have to sign in as much detail as required to make sure you understand the process completely.

In particular, we will review all the numbers on the Vendor's Statement of Adjustments to ensure they are correct to the best of your knowledge (for instance, that the property tax adjustment is based on the amount of property taxes that you actually paid). Having said that, when you are selling a property the appointment will normally be much shorter than if you are buying a property.

Insurance Coverage

In addition, I will tell you that although we have reminded you to cancel your insurance coverage, you want to be sure we have received sale proceeds and that the transaction has, in fact completed, before the insurance coverage is actually cancelled.

This is because insurance coverage is only valid if you are the registered owner of a property so even if the buyer has arranged for insurance coverage for the property, if there is a delay in completion you need to ensure that your insurance coverage will still be in place until the transfer actually takes place. Accordingly, I usually recommend that you cancel your insurance effective two or three days after the scheduled completion date.

Transfer of Keys

I will also tell you that you need to give keys to your property to your real estate agent so that they may be passed on to the buyer. However, you want to be sure that the keys do not get passed on before completion has occurred. Most real estate agents will be reluctant to hand over keys until they have received confirmation from at least one of the participating law firms that the transfer has been registered and sale funds have been delivered.

On occasion, however, a situation will arise where a buyer will ask for early possession of the property, either because you have already vacated the premises and the buyer can get an early start on the move-in process, or because there has been a delay in completion but the buyer, who is also selling his current home, needs to vacate the same.

My advice is to never grant early possession to a buyer. This is not because I am a mean lawyer, but because it is very hard to protect you if you have turned over the keys early. In rare cases, I will work with a seller to grant early possession by having the buyer sign a rental agreement. This will at least give you some rights under the Residential Tenancy legislation in your jurisdiction to evict your tenant, and perhaps even take possession of some of your tenant's goods, for failure to pay. Without a tenancy agreement you may find it very difficult to evict the buyer if he doesn't come up with sale proceeds within a reasonable time.

Returning Documents

Once you have signed the documents, I will return them to the buyer's lawyer, placing her on undertakings not to use the documents in any way until she has in her trust account all the funds that she requires to complete the transaction, with the exception of any mortgage proceeds which the buyer may be getting (but also that she and the buyer have complied with all the lender's requirements such that once the mortgage document has been registered, the mortgage lender will be compelled to advance the mortgage funds).

Many mortgage lenders require that a mortgage be registered before they will actually advance the proceeds. Accordingly, it is important that the buyer's lawyer be permitted to register the documents before actually having the mortgage proceeds in her trust account. From a seller's perspective, however, it is important that the buyer's lawyer have all other funds required to complete the transaction in trust prior to registering the documents as you do not want the title to the property to transfer to the buyer's name without absolute assurance that you will receive your sale proceeds.

The corollary to this is that you, as the seller, though having agreed to transfer the title to the property to the buyer free and clear of all financial encumbrances, need to be able to receive sale proceeds before having to repay those financial encumbrances. This is what makes it so vital that in British Columbia our real estate conveyancing be completed based on lawyer's undertakings, or promises. So long as I undertake to use the sale proceeds to repay and discharge the financial encumbrances registered against the property, the buyer's lawyer will send sale proceeds to my office, knowing that those encumbrances will be paid out and discharged).

Receipt and Payout of Funds

Mortgage Payout

On the date scheduled for completion, I will receive funds from the buyer's lawyer, hopefully early enough to allow me to complete my payout process without incurring additional interest. Many lenders require funds to reach their office prior to a certain time (usually somewhere between 1:00 p.m. and 3:00 p.m.) or they will charge interest on your mortgage repayment amount until the next business day.

Accordingly, I will normally have all of my letters and other completion documents prepared in advance and ready to be sent out immediately upon receipt of funds. Funds are sent to the lender, along with a Form C Release of Mortgage document, on the trust condition that the lender will apply the funds to the repayment in full of your mortgage debt, and that the lender will sign and return to my office the Form C Release of Mortgage document in order that we can register that document in the Land Title Office to remove that encumbrance from the title to the property.

Real Estate Fees

In addition to paying out your financial encumbrances, I will pay the real estate fees owing to the real estate agents that listed and sold your property (and will provide them with a letter by fax and often a telephone call to confirm that completion has taken place and keys may be delivered to the buyer).

Other Payouts

I will also pay any other incidental expenses such as the cost of obtaining strata documents required for completion, any outstanding property taxes or utility accounts or strata fees, and, of course, my legal fees and disbursements for acting for you in this matter.

Document Package

I will also put together a package of documents for you, including a copy of the Vendor's Statement of Adjustments, Order to Pay, copies of letters enclosing payments made on your behalf (for example, a copy of the letter to your mortgage lender enclosing the proceeds required to pay out and obtain a discharge of your mortgage), a Trust Reconciliation Statement and a copy of our Statement of Account.

The Trust Reconciliation Statement will show details of all the money we received (usually just sale proceeds from the buyer's lawyer but this may also include excess deposit funds if the amount of the deposit exceeded the amount of real estate fee payable to the real estate company which was holding the deposit), as well as details of all the money we paid out on your behalf, including the sale proceeds payable to you. Any money owing to you will be provided by way of either a cheque drawn to your order or by way of a deposit to your bank account.

Post-Completion Matters

After you have received your completion package from my office, you will likely not hear from me again regarding this transaction, however, my job is not yet over. I am still required to follow up with any mortgage lender you were dealing with to ensure that they send me the signed Form C Release document and, upon receipt of that document, I will register the same at the Land Title Office.

Finally, I will report to the buyer's lawyer with the registration number of the Form C Release and, only once all this has been completed, I am in a position to close my file.

Appendix A *

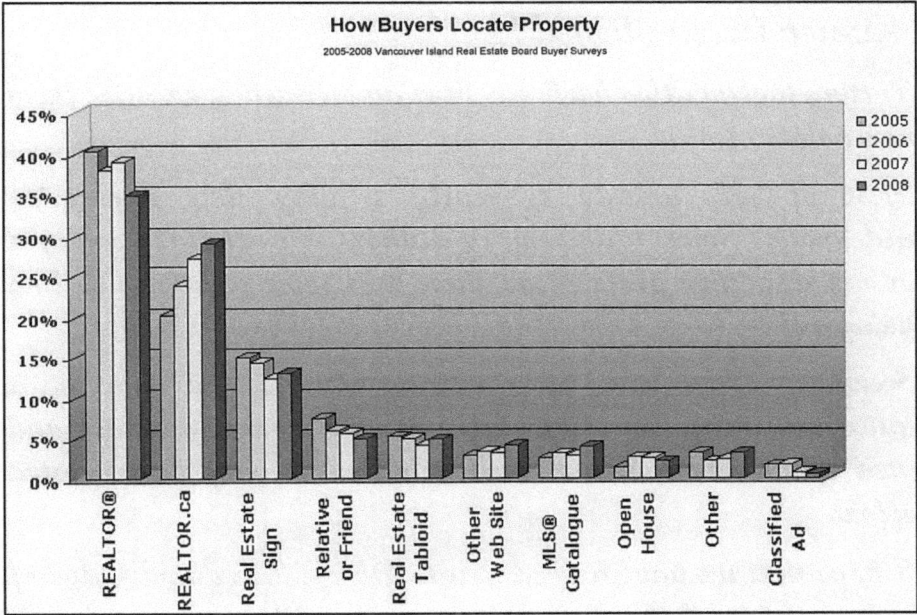

How Buyers Locate Property
2005-2008 Vancouver Island Real Estate Board Buyer Surveys

Legend: 2005, 2006, 2007, 2008

Y-axis: 0%, 5%, 10%, 15%, 20%, 25%, 30%, 35%, 40%, 45%

X-axis categories: REALTOR®, REALTOR.ca, Real Estate Sign, Relative or Friend, Real Estate Tabloid, Other Web Site, MLS® Catalogue, Open House, Other, Classified Ad

*2005-2008 Vancouver Island Real Estate Board Buyer Surveys

A Final Word

Mission Accomplished !

Putting together this book has been an interesting exercise from two points of view.

First of all, writing is really a very time consuming endeavour. Since I, and my co-authors, are all fully engaged in our respective professions, there was some creative juggling going on!

Secondly, after years of practicing what we do -- we do it quite naturally. So to break the process down into steps and then to write out those steps required a very concentrated effort.

I hope that we have helped you to have a better knowledge of some aspects of the real estate process. We can't answer all the questions but we hope we increased your understanding.

When you are contemplating buying or selling, engage the professionals in the real estate dialogue. You need to know so ask the questions.

Thank you to my co-authors Kelly, Robert and Josée. You were great on this project and a pleasure to work with. I also admire you in your respective professions.

To the readers, I thank you for taking the time to check out our discussions.

If your real estate needs are in the Greater Victoria area of

BC, give us a call. We would be delighted to help you. You already know us to some degree so don't hesitate to get in touch.

Vi Brown